JAZZ UKULELE
MASTERY 1

UKELIKETHEPROS
© 2024 TERRY CARTER

ISBN-13: **9-781958-192108**
UKELIKETHEPROS.COM
© 2024 TERRY CARTER

TABLE OF CONTENTS

Jazz Ukulele Mastery	01
Triplet Counting	04
Triplets Exercises	05
Swing vs. Straight	07
Strumming Patterns - Exercise A	08
Strumming Patterns - Exercise B	08
Strumming Patterns - Exercise C	09
Open Position Voicings	10
Closed Position Voicings	11
Show Strokes	13
Left Hand Muting	15
Split Stroke - Exercise A	17
Split Stroke - Exercise B	18
Split Stroke - Exercise C	19
Split Stroke - Exercise D	20
Swing Etude - A1 Section	21
Swing Etude - A2 Section	22
Swing Etude - B Section	23
Swing Etude - A3 Section	24
Swing Etude	25
Great Job!	29
The Essentials	A
How To Read Tab	B
Notes On The Ukulele Neck	C
Ukulele Hands	D
Ukulele Parts	E
Understanding Chord Diagrams	F
Chord Chart	G
Music Symbols To Know	I
About The Publisher	K
About Uke Like The Pros	L
About Terry Carter Music Store	M

JAZZ UKULELE
MASTERY 1

Welcome to a musical expedition like no other, where the spirited syncopations of Jazz intertwine with the melodic charm of the ukulele. In this book, Jazz Ukulele Mastery 1, we'll present you a series designed to immerse you in the captivating world of Jazz Ukulele, from the hands of Christopher Davis-Shannon and Uke Like The Pros. This journey is not just about learning chords and techniques; it's about exploring a rich musical history and the unique place the ukulele holds within it.

Jazz, with its roots deeply embedded in the African American communities of New Orleans, blossomed in the early 20th century into a formidable genre that would influence music worldwide. It was an era of innovation and cultural synthesis, where the sounds of ragtime, blues, and African music melded together to create something entirely new and exhilarating. As Jazz spread its wings from the bustling streets of New Orleans to the vibrant speakeasies of Chicago and New York, it carried with it a spirit of freedom and creativity.

The ukulele, originally introduced to the Hawaiian Islands by Portuguese immigrants, found a unique voice within the Jazz movement. By the 1920s and '30s, the ukulele had become a symbol of the Jazz Age, capturing the era's exuberance and its penchant for experimentation. Musicians like Roy Smeck and Johnny Marvin not only showcased the ukulele's versatility but also its ability to convey the complexity and vibrancy of Jazz. Across the pond, George Formby introduced the banjo uke to British audiences, further cementing the instrument's place in the annals of Jazz history.

In this series, we'll dive into the heart of swing style uke playing, a style that thrived from the '20s until the early '40s and continues to enchant to this day. We'll explore the idiochromatic voicings and the nuanced right-hand techniques that define this genre, drawing inspiration from the greats who paved the way. Through lessons crafted for both beginners and seasoned players, we aim to connect you not only with the techniques required to master the Jazz Ukulele but with the stories and personalities that have shaped its legacy.

So, as we embark on this journey together, we'll not only be learning how to play the ukulele in a Jazz style but also celebrating the rich tapestry of history that accompanies each strum and chord change. From the smoky Jazz clubs of yesteryear to the resurgence of the ukulele in modern music, our exploration will be as much about connecting with the past as it is about creating new sounds and memories. With your ukulele in hand, let's begin this journey into the heart of Jazz, where each note tells a story and every song is a step back in time.

So, grab your ukulele, open your heart and soul, and let's dive into the magical world of Jazz Ukulele. Let's create music that not only sounds beautiful but also resonates with the Jazz ancestors. Welcome to your Jazz Ukulele Mastery 1 course, brought to you by Uke Like The Pros and Christopher Davis-Shannon. Let's get started!

CHRISTOPHER DAVIS-SHANNON

Christopher Davis-Shannon, residing in London, is celebrated both for his exceptional skills as a ukulele performer and his dedication as an educator. Known for his unique style that blends influences from a variety of ukulele masters, Davis-Shannon stands out in ukulele festivals worldwide, captivating audiences with his performances that traverse genres from the great American songbook, Hawaiian standards, to Brazilian bossa nova, alongside his original compositions. His intricate right-hand techniques and harmonic ingenuity have crafted a signature ukulele sound that is both timeless and distinctly his.

Beyond his performances, Davis-Shannon has made significant contributions as an educator. He is a sought-after private tutor and clinician, known for his workshops at festivals and folk music organizations. His educational materials cover a wide range of techniques and theories, including baroque campanella, clawhammer banjo adaptations, and rhythmic studies on George Formby. Additionally, his articles on chord theory and rhythm have been featured in numerous ukulele publications. Christopher's compositions, ranging from songs reminiscent of the great American songbook to pieces influenced by classical minimalist ideals, are highlighted in his latest album FIFTY/50, which showcases a collaboration with accordionist Jaques Pellarin.

TRIPLET COUNTING

The triplet rhythm, or subdivision, is the heart and soul of swing music. This subdivision of the beat into three equal parts is the foundation of rhythm. Feeling this is an important first step to playing the music. When clapping these rhythms try to tap your foot on the downbeats (1-2-3-4) while slapping and saying the triplet rhythm.

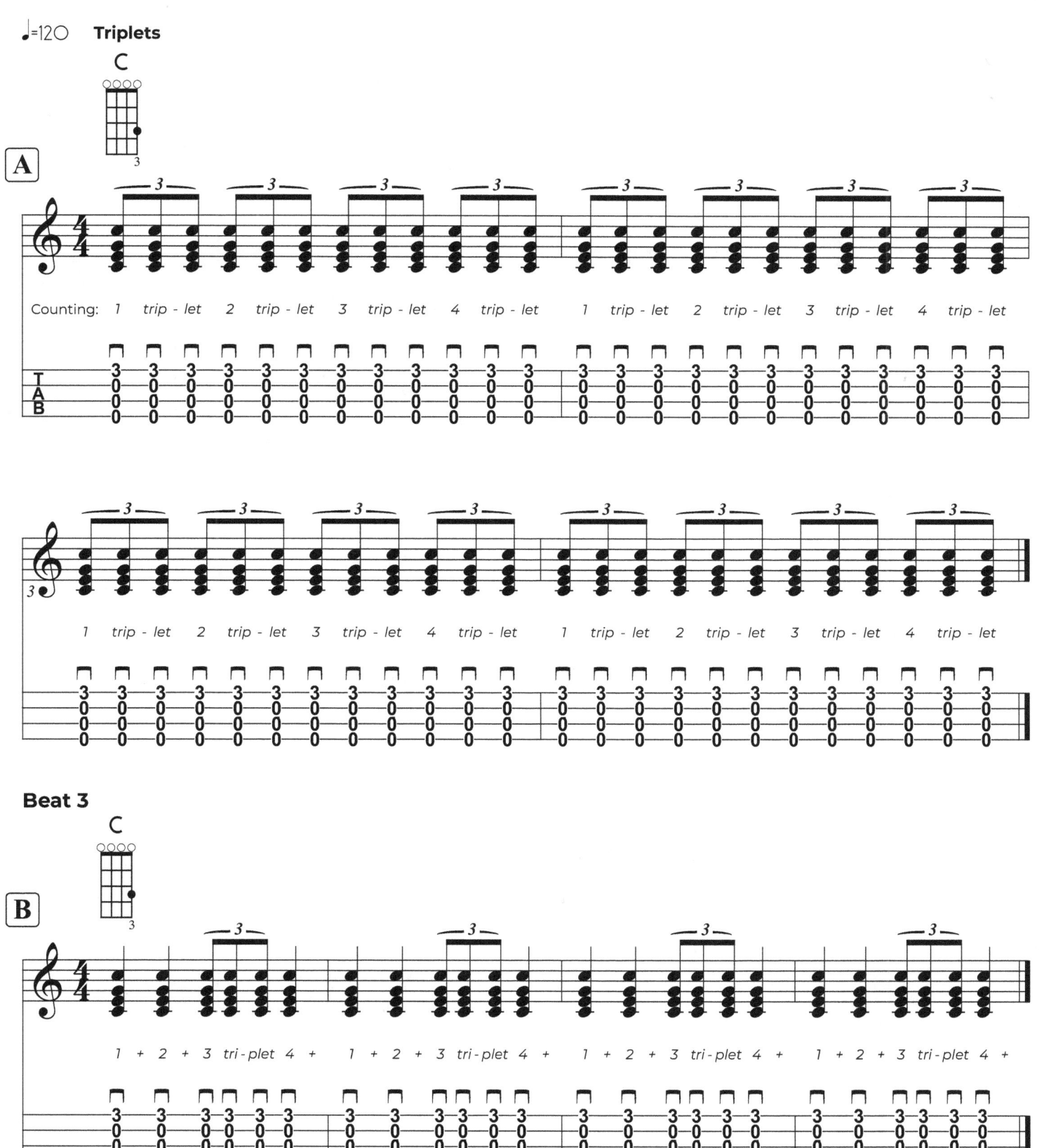

TRIPLETS EXERCISES
PG. 1 of 2

While there are many ways to play the triplet rhythm on ukulele, the thumb roll triplet is the most commonly used as it relies on our basic down and up motion of strumming. For each triplet strum down with your index finger, followed by the thumb, and complete the motion with an upstrum. Practice slowly at first to keep the triplets even. This can take some time at first but soon they'll be rolling out on any beat naturally.

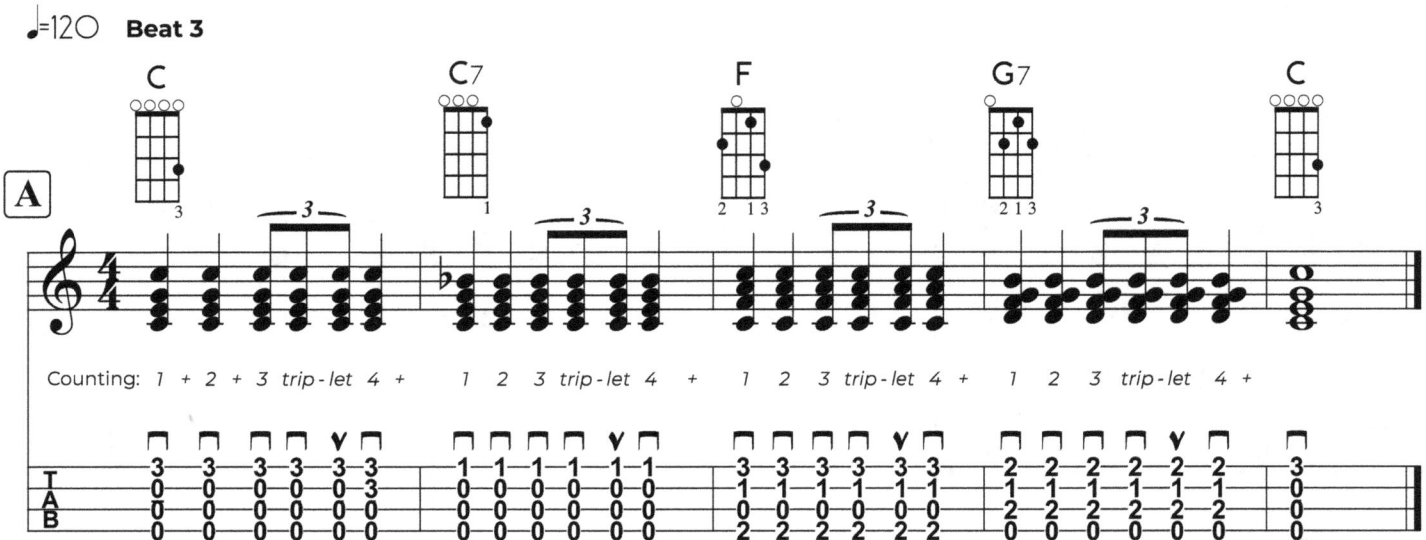

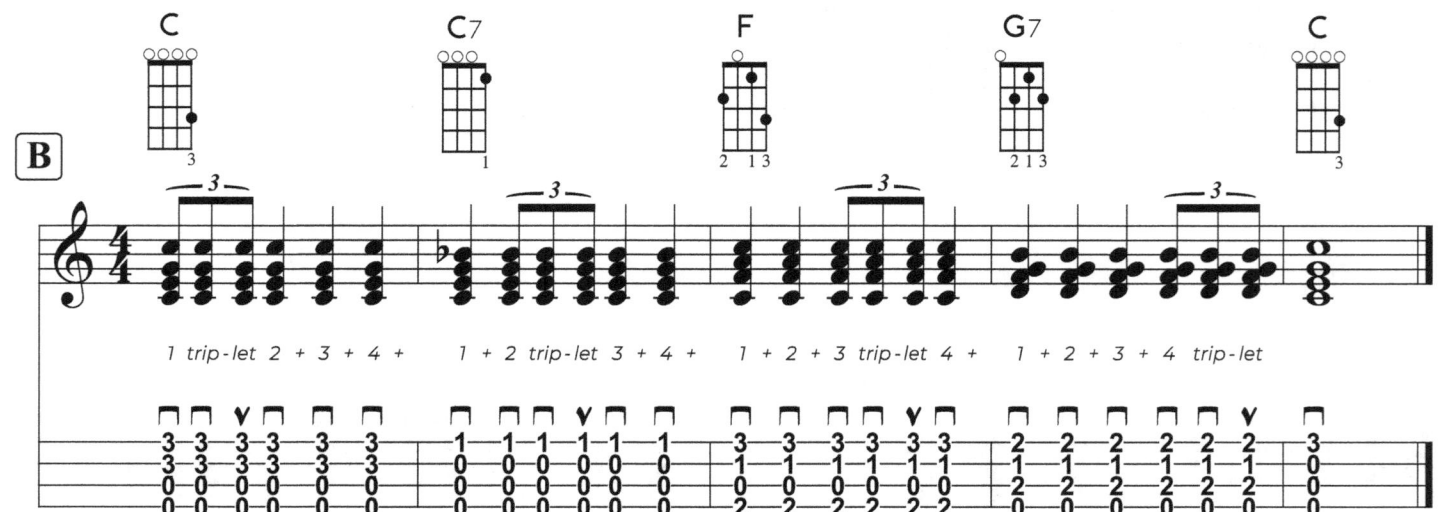

TRIPLETS EXERCISES
PG. 2 of 2

Mix it Up

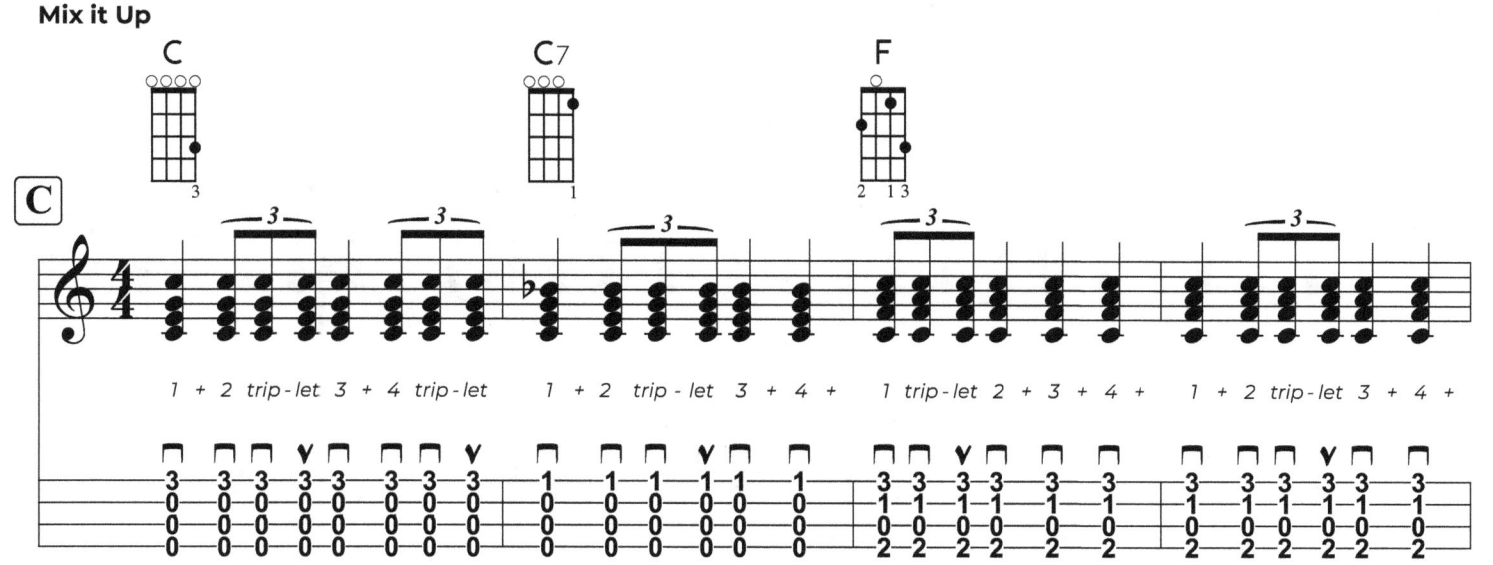

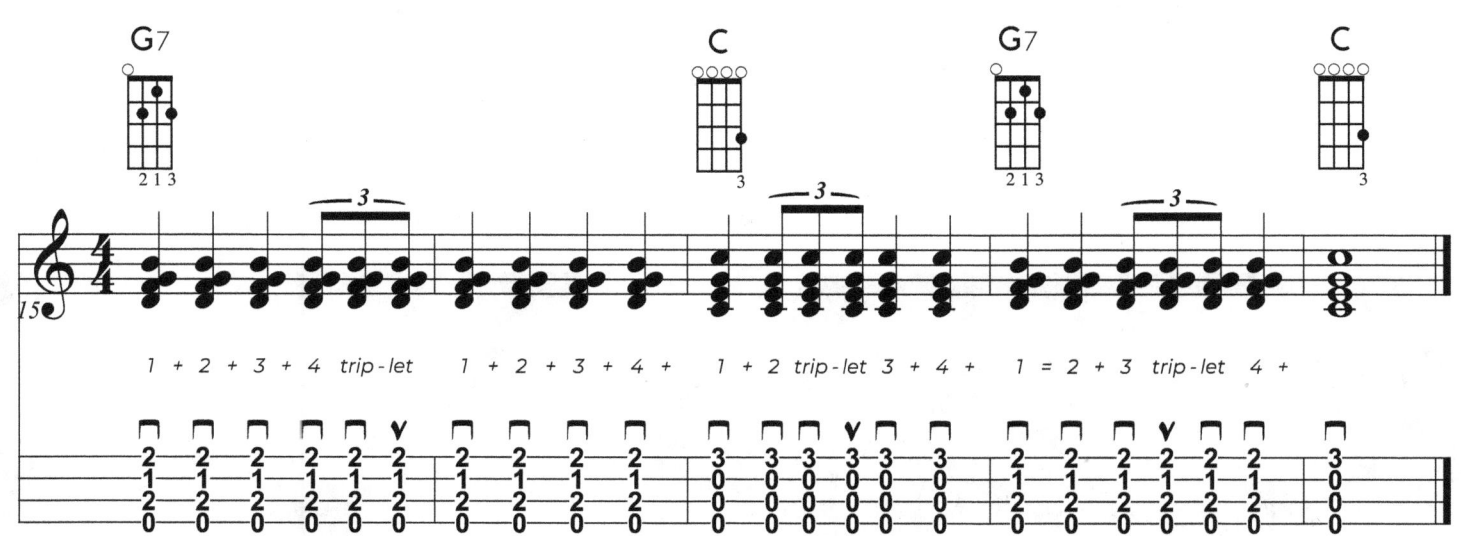

SWING vs STRAIGHT

Now that we can feel the triplet rhythm, it's time to look at how that is our building block for the up strum. Eighth notes are half of the beat but in this style are 'swung' or have a long short feel. You can feel the basis of this by playing your triplet but omitting the down strum with the thumb. This is a good starting point for feeling the swung eighth note but keep in mind that every player has their own concept of feel. The best way to learn this is to listen to musicians from the 1930s and 40s to hear how they played eighth notes and find your own personal space within that.

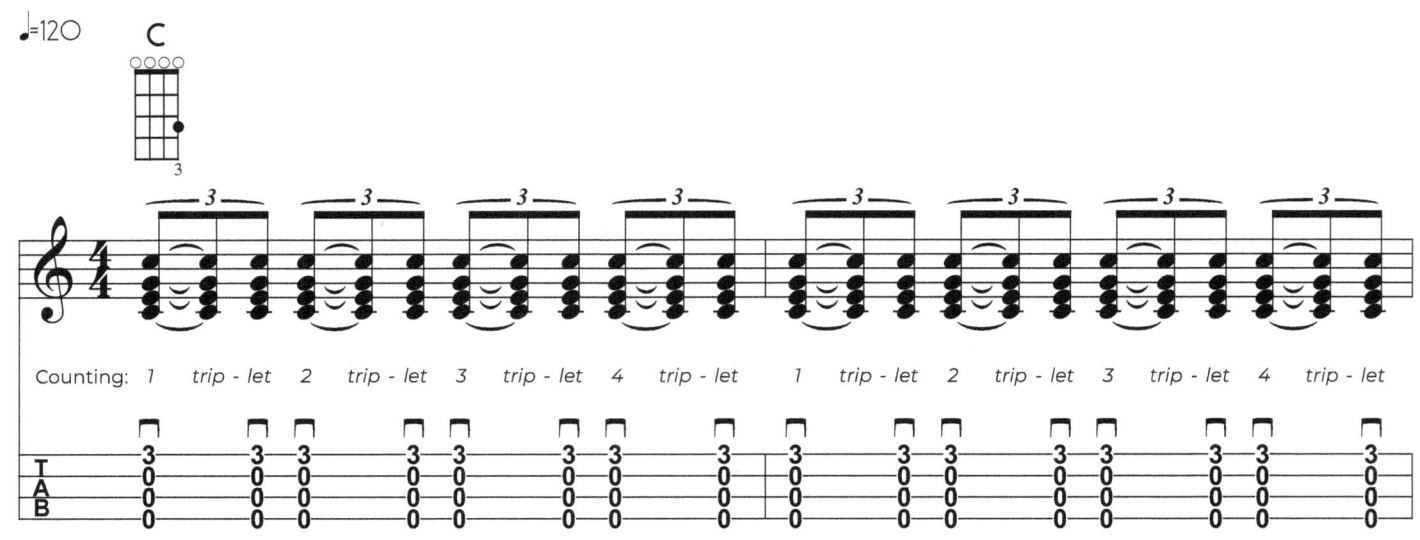

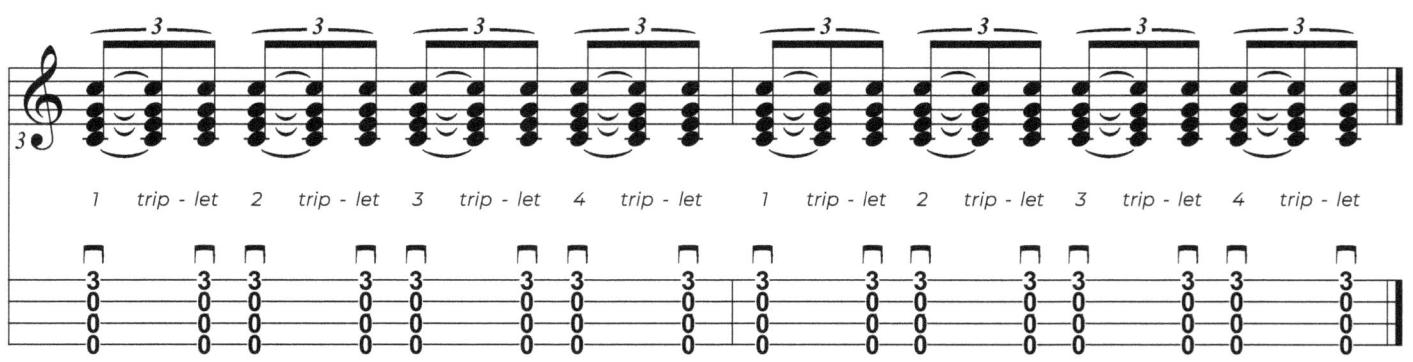

ALL YOUR MUSIC NEEDS
TERRYCARTERMUSICSTORE.COM

STRUMMING PATTERNS
EXERCISE - A

Now that we feel that triplet it's time to strip it away and think about the most basic form of strumming - quarter note down strums. Keep that triplet feel in our head and strum down with the index finger on each beat. Remember to strum quickly through the strings, not hard, but fast!

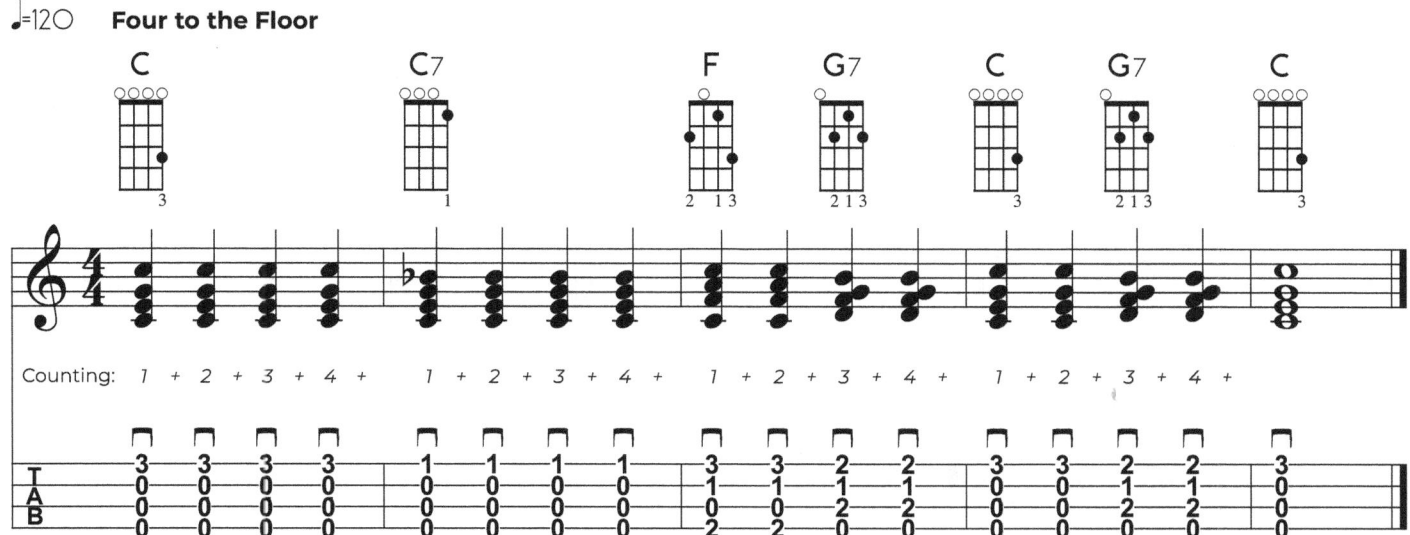

STRUMMING PATTERNS
EXERCISE - B

Time to add in some up strums while keeping in mind that these are swung eighth notes. In this exercise we're adding a few down- up strums to our down strum pattern to create a bit more rhythmic variety. Let the up strums be lighter than the down strums with the pad of the finger. If you don't happen to hit all of the notes on the up strum that is fine. The down strums are always our pulse.

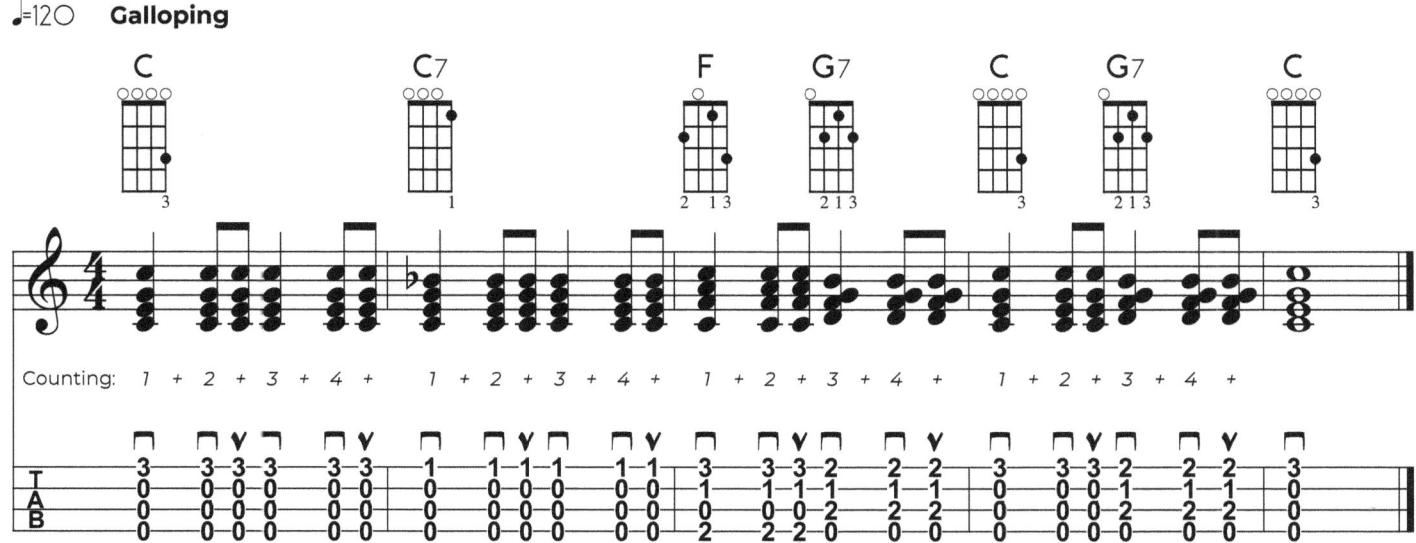

STRUMMING PATTERNS
EXERCISE - C

The shuffle pattern brings in all swung eighth notes or down- up strums. Keep in mind that the down strums are always the most important. Think of a train rolling down the tracks for the shuffle strum - Long, Short, Long, Short. Give a little accent on beats 2 and 4 to really hammer home the swing rhythm. Now is the time to start stepping away from set strumming patterns and think about all these variations of the down and up strum as a toolbox for us to choose from. As long as the pulse is there we can play up strums any time that we choose. Let feel guide you when you play vs getting stuck in the strumming pattern trap.

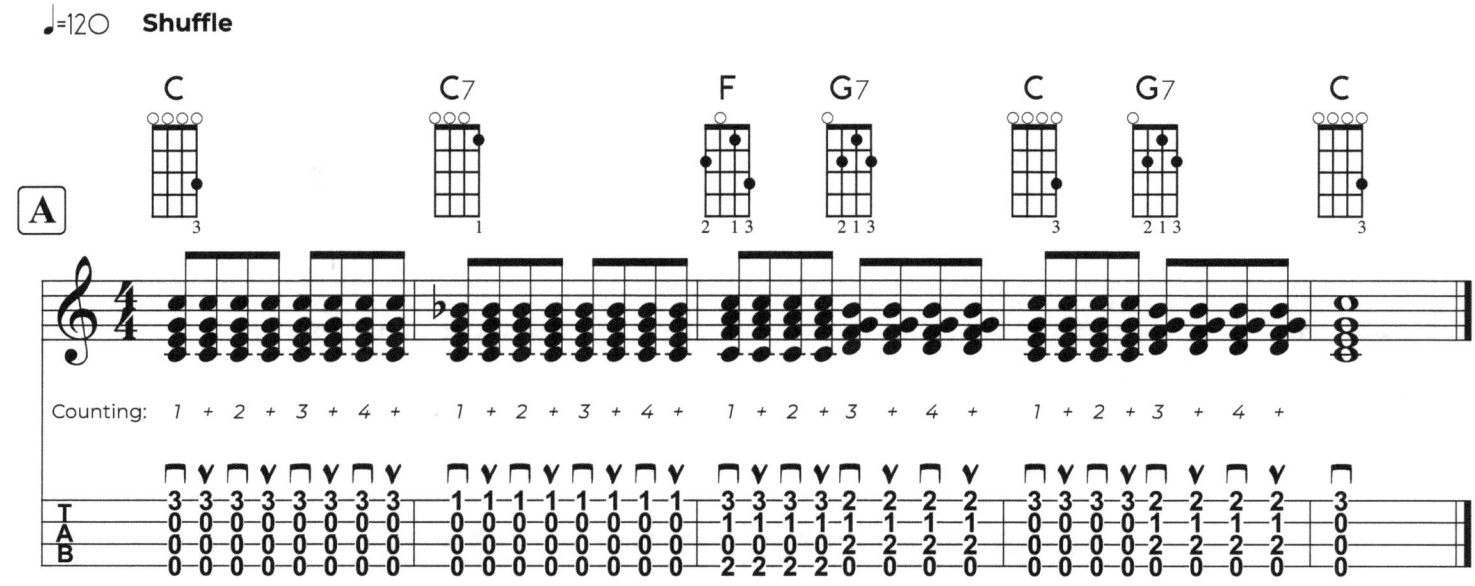

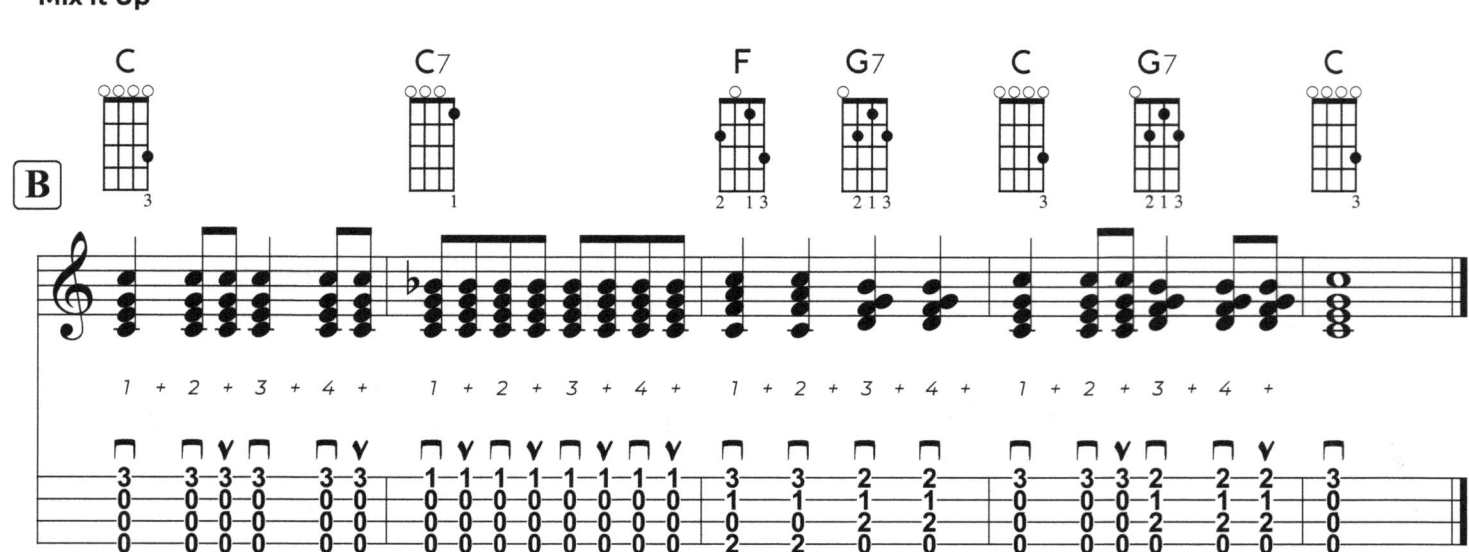

OPEN POSITION VOICINGS

Open Position chords are our chords on ukulele that use our open strings. These are commonly the first chords that we use and should look familiar to most players. You'll note a few slight changes to the standard chords - most notably that the F uses the pinky on the A string to play a C. This creates a fuller sounding chord than our open A string but is also optional. All F's are created equal so feel free to use whatever F chord is most natural to you.

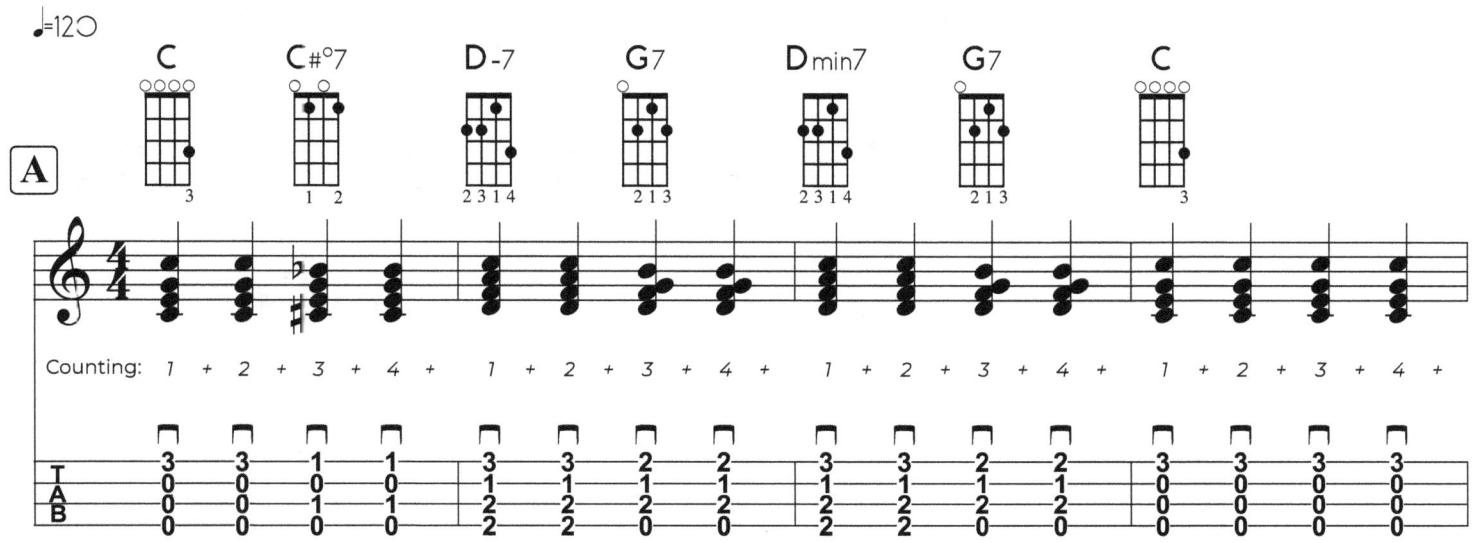

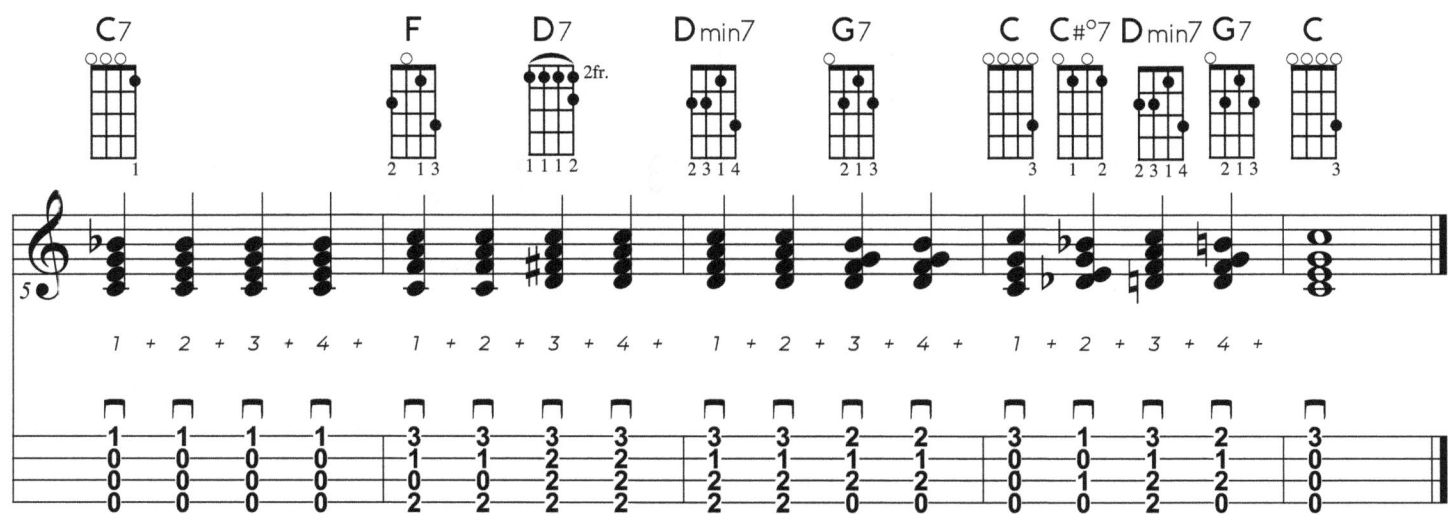

CLOSED POSITION VOICINGS

Once you have the open position chords under your fingers it's time to start moving them on up the neck. Let's play the same exact chords but with no open strings. Take note that the F6 and Dm7 are the same exact chord, that's the beauty of music! Some of these chords may seem tough to play at first but take your time to get them under your fingers as once you can make the shape they are all moveable and will give you 12 chords in one!

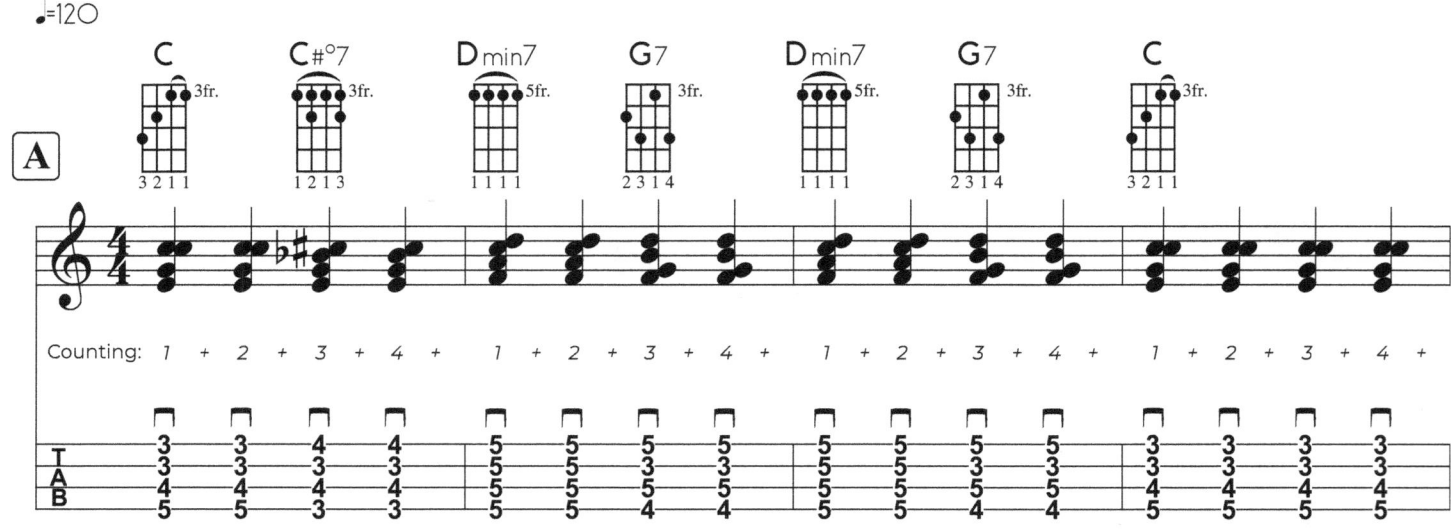

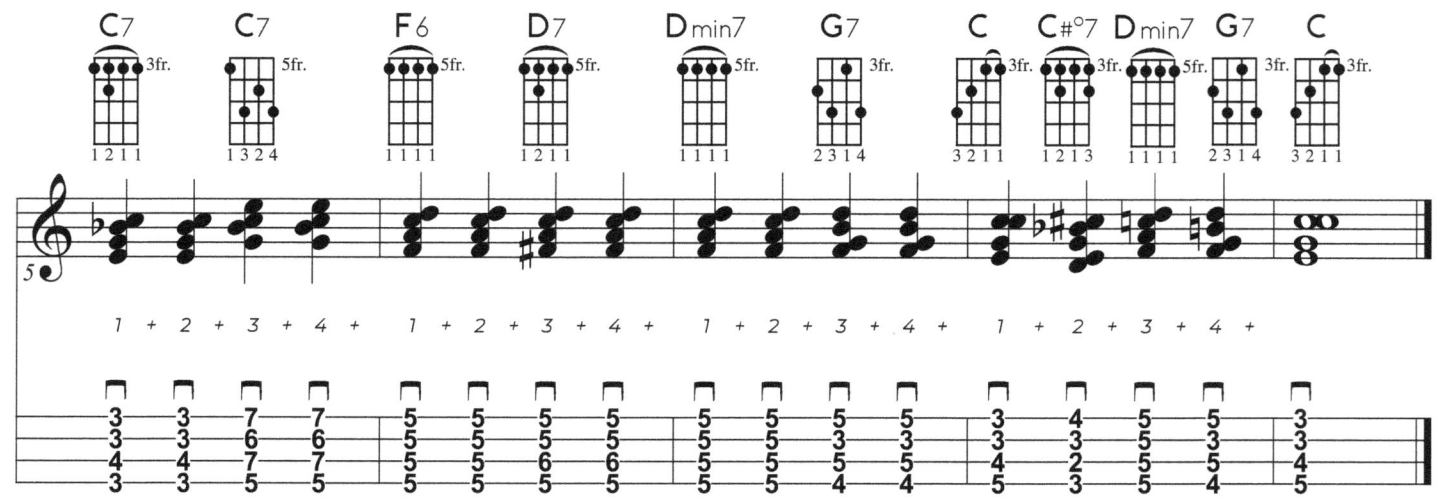

SHOW STROKES
(Figure Eight & Winding the Clock)

PG. 1 of 2

The Figure Eight and Winding the Clock are two exaggerated motions Roy Smeck would use for visual appeal. When winding the clock play down and up strums but make a big circle on your ukulele, get as close to your hands with the downstroke and close to the bridge as possible with the up stroke for maximum effect!

SHOW STROKES
PG. 2 of 2

Figure Eight

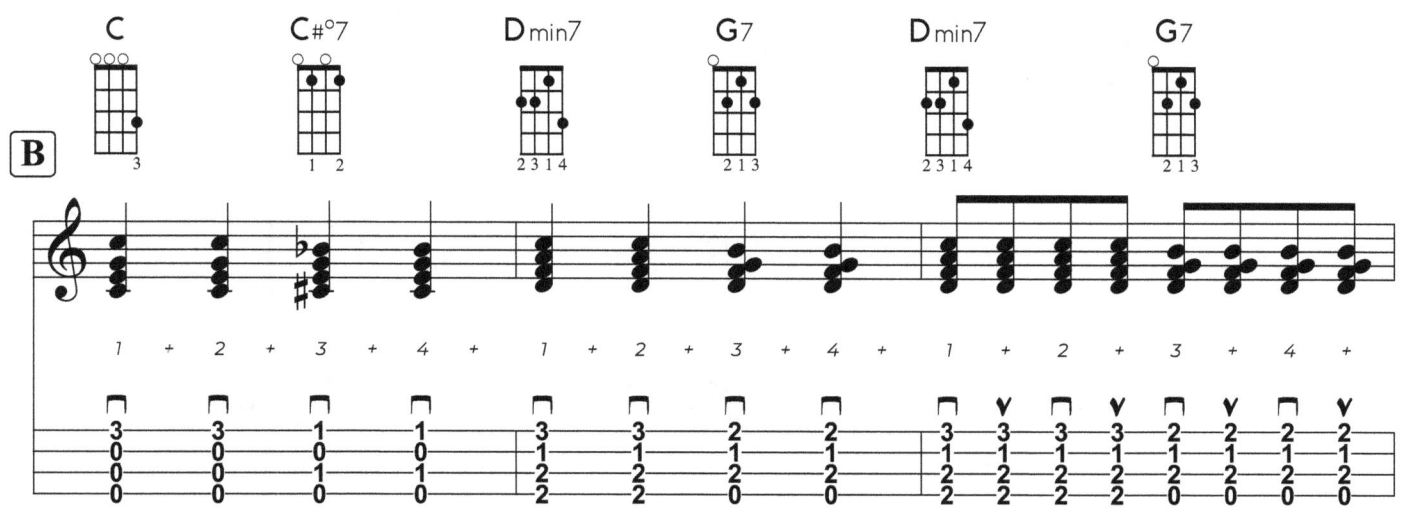
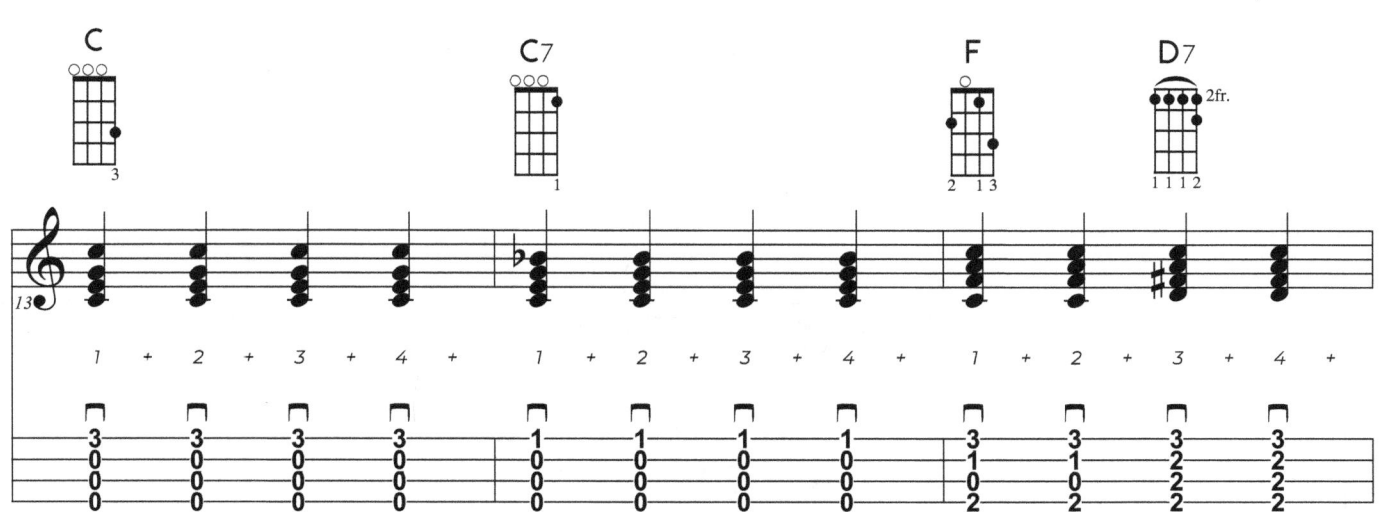
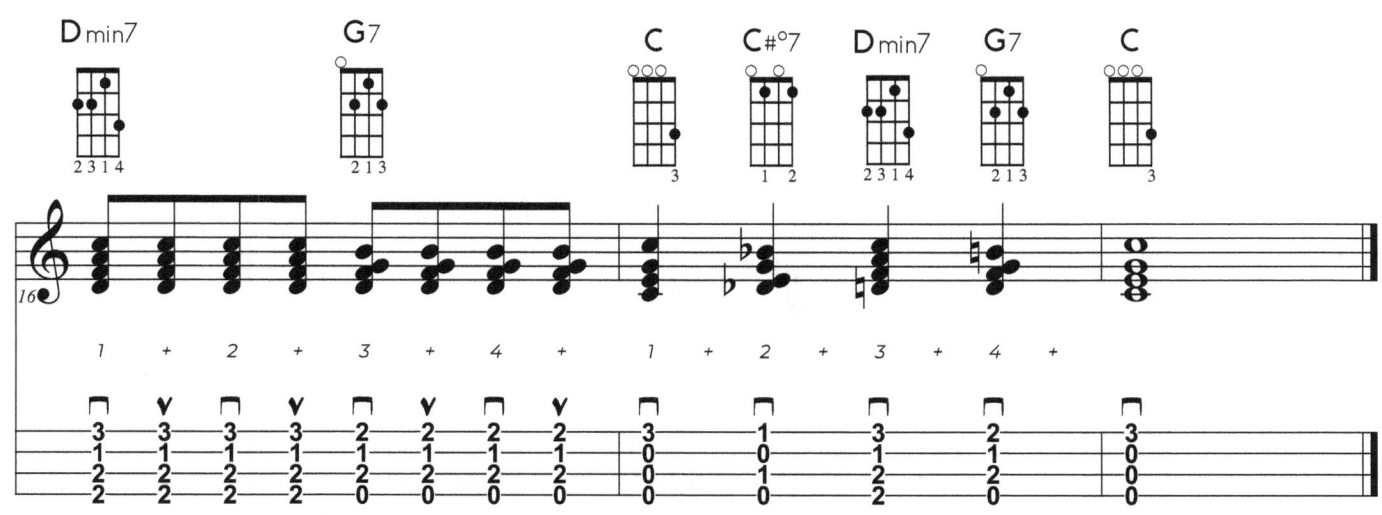

LEFT HAND MUTING

PG. 1 of 2

Start by playing a chord and then gently releasing pressure, not fully lifting up the finger, to stop the sound. Be sure that the sound stops entirely without buzzing. Once you are comfortable doing this once per measure move on to exercise B playing two chords with space per measure. Then finally you can go back to the closed position chord exercise and practice putting a little space in between each chord creating a little breathing room between strums.

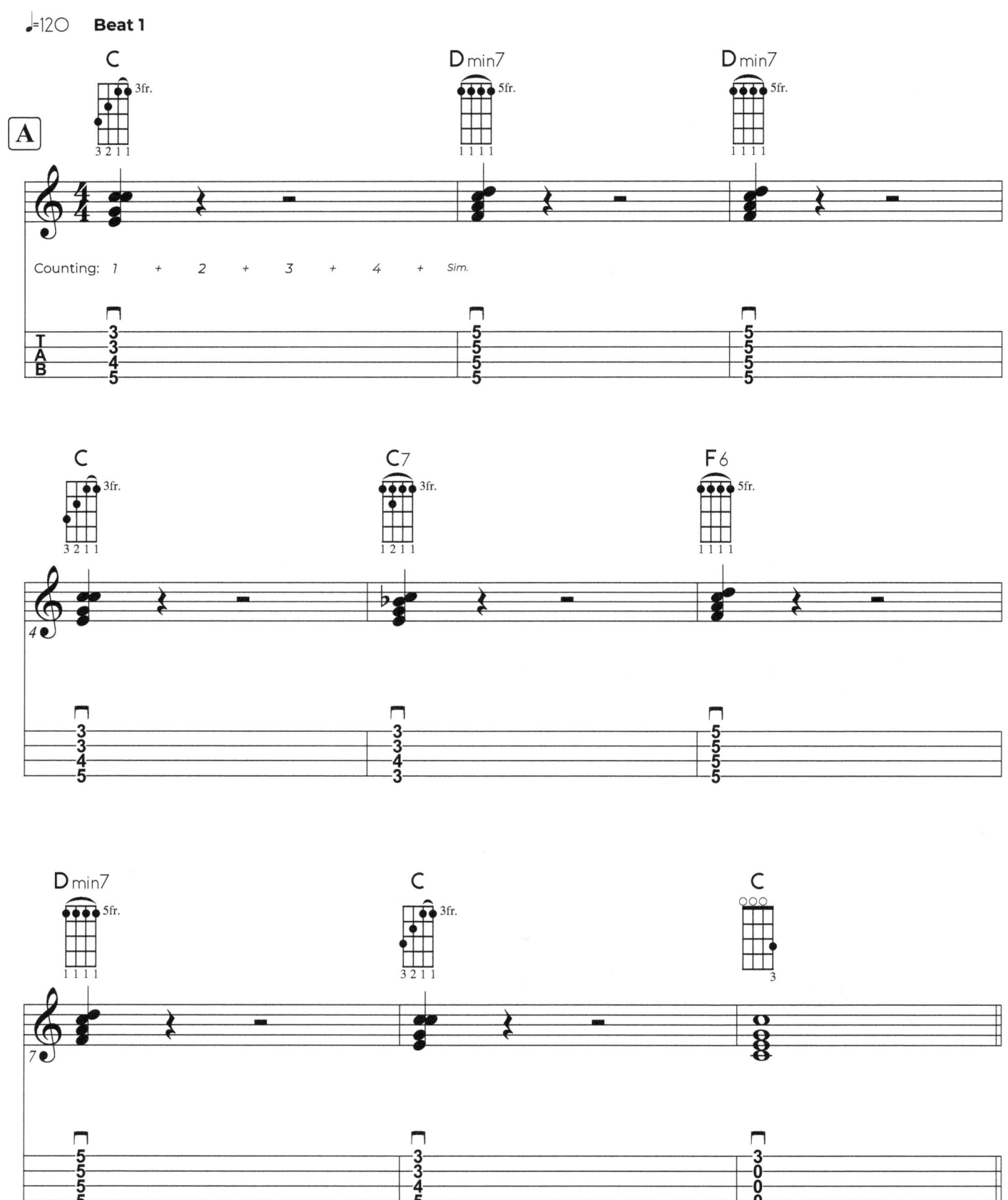

LEFT HAND MUTING
PG. 2 of 2

SPLIT STROKE
EXERCISE - A

The split stroke is a challenging technique that allows us to play unique rhythms as well as melodies on ukulele. The split stroke really consists of playing two rhythms at once and in the first exercise we look at the clave rhythm. These will be all of the full down strums in our total split stroke pattern. Clap along with the exercise and internalize that rhythm before applying the chords.

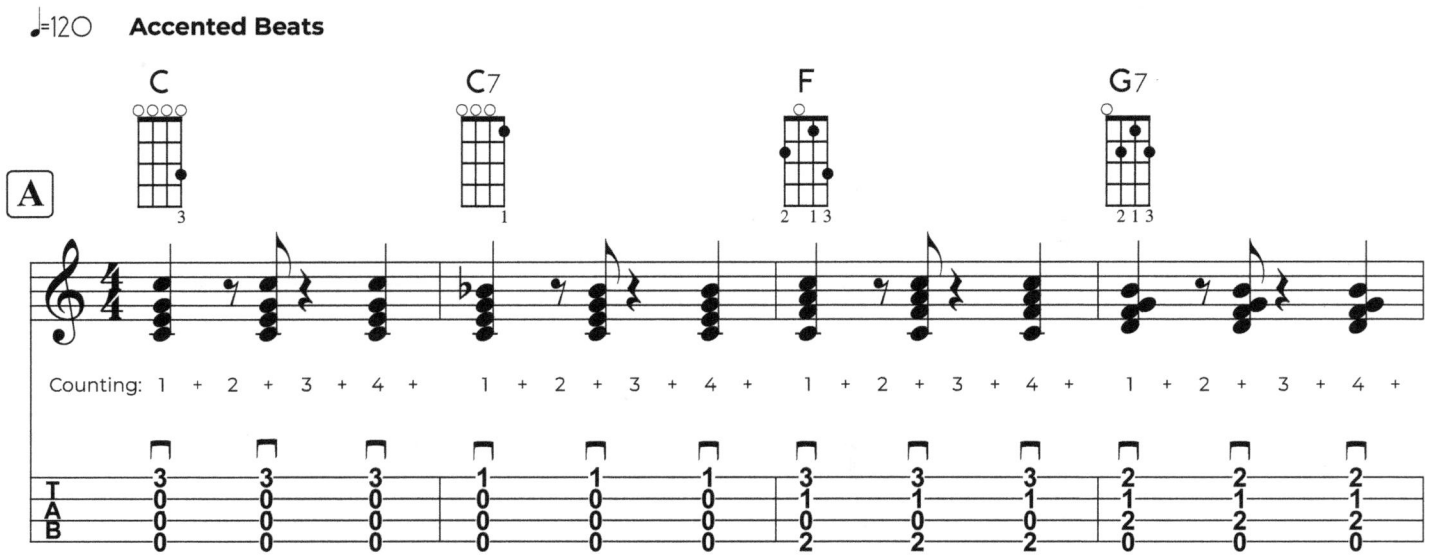

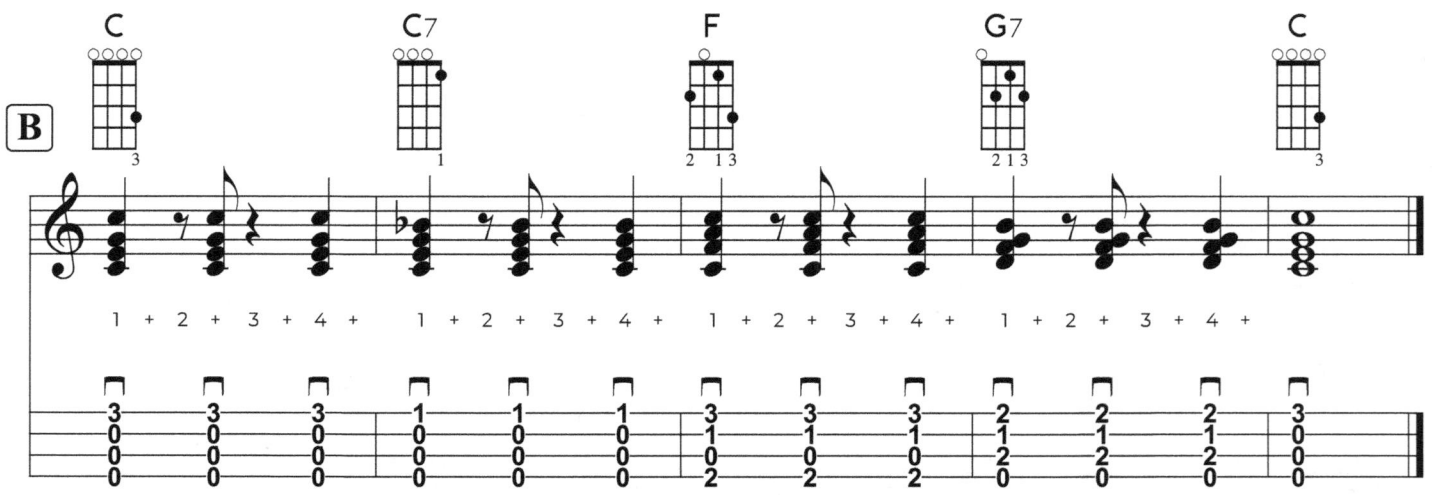

SPLIT STROKE
EXERCISE - B

Now it's time to add in the strumming pattern itself and this is where things can start to feel awkward for many players. While we play straight eighth notes the strumming patterns give us a very specific accent pattern: the clave. Pay close attention to the strumming motions in this lesson and practice them with muted strums first without chords. Slow and steady wins the race!

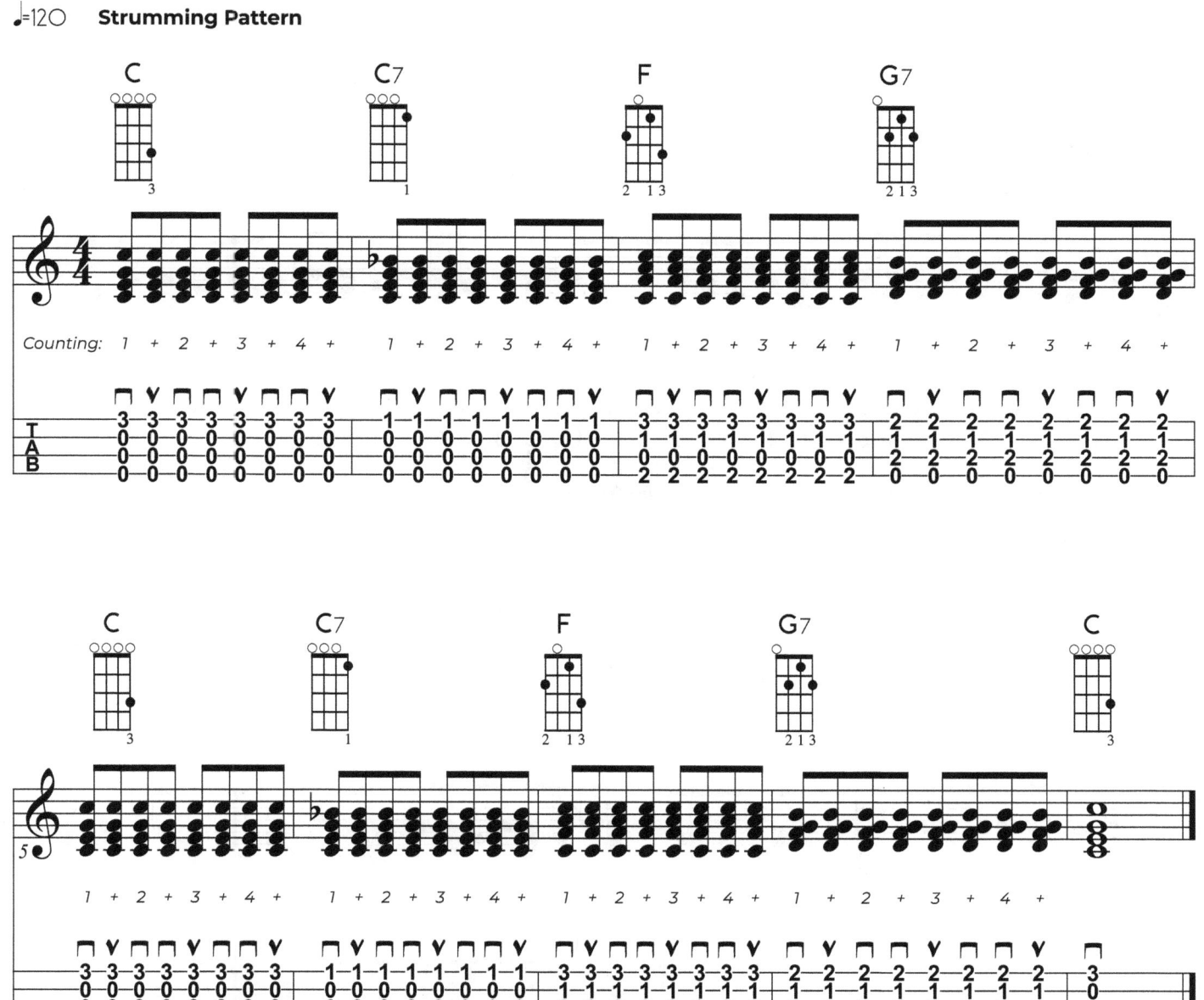

SPLIT STROKE
EXERCISE - C

The key to the split stroke is isolating the notes on the A and G strings creating a moving melody line. In this strumming pattern each upstroke hits only the A string (or as close as we can to that!) and in each grouping of double down strokes we bounce off of the G string. This now lets us hear our full down strums on the clave rhythm while playing a moving melody line over top. When starting out, I find it helpful to say the motions your hand is making as the strumming pattern can be quite confusing.

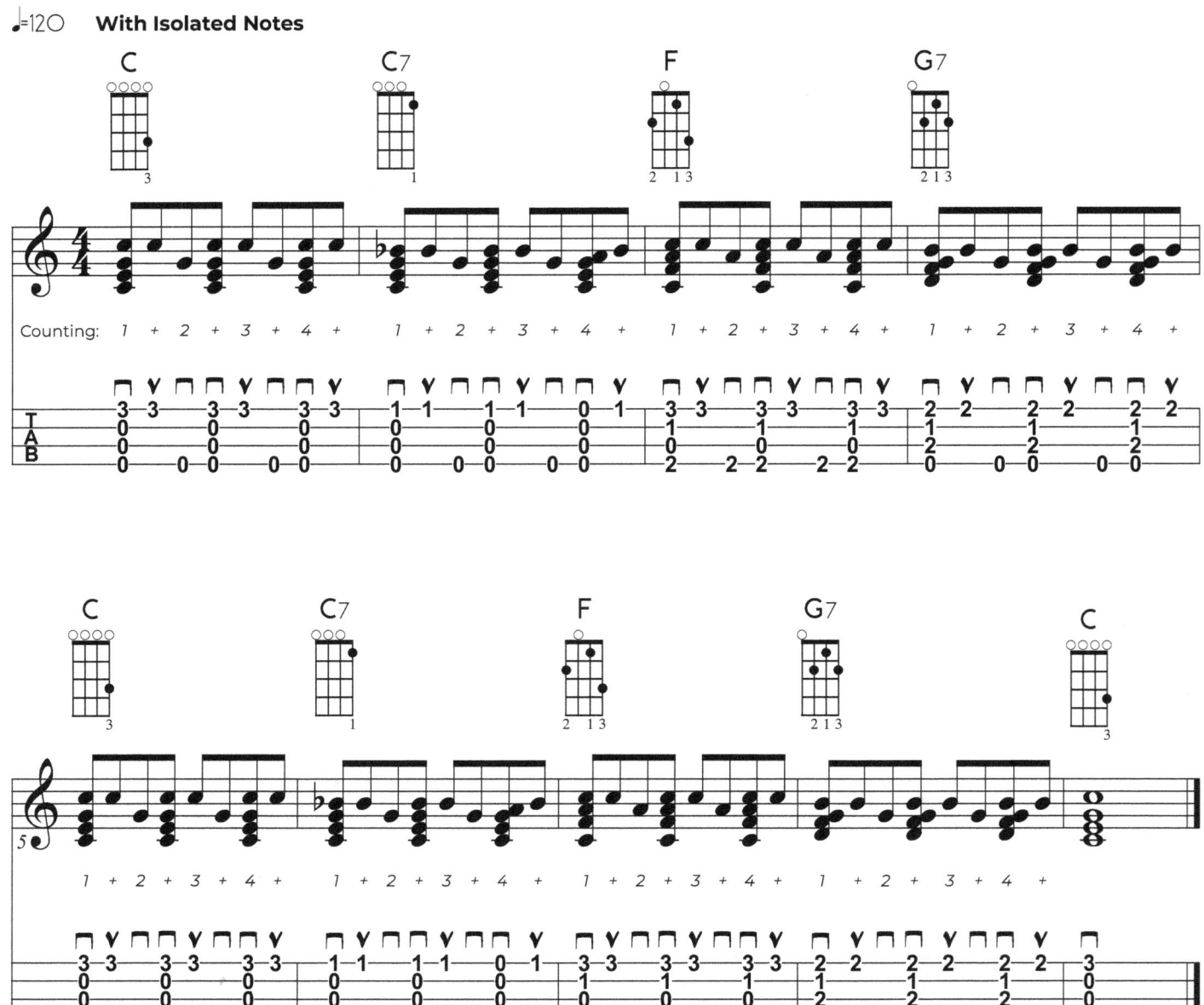

SPLIT STROKE
EXERCISE - D

In our final split stroke exercise we add finger lifts. To give more movement to the melody we can lift up our finger and occasionally play an open A string over any chord. On every upstream lift up your finger and put it down for the next down strum. Playing this slowly you can hear the simple melody created between the two outer strings of the instrument.

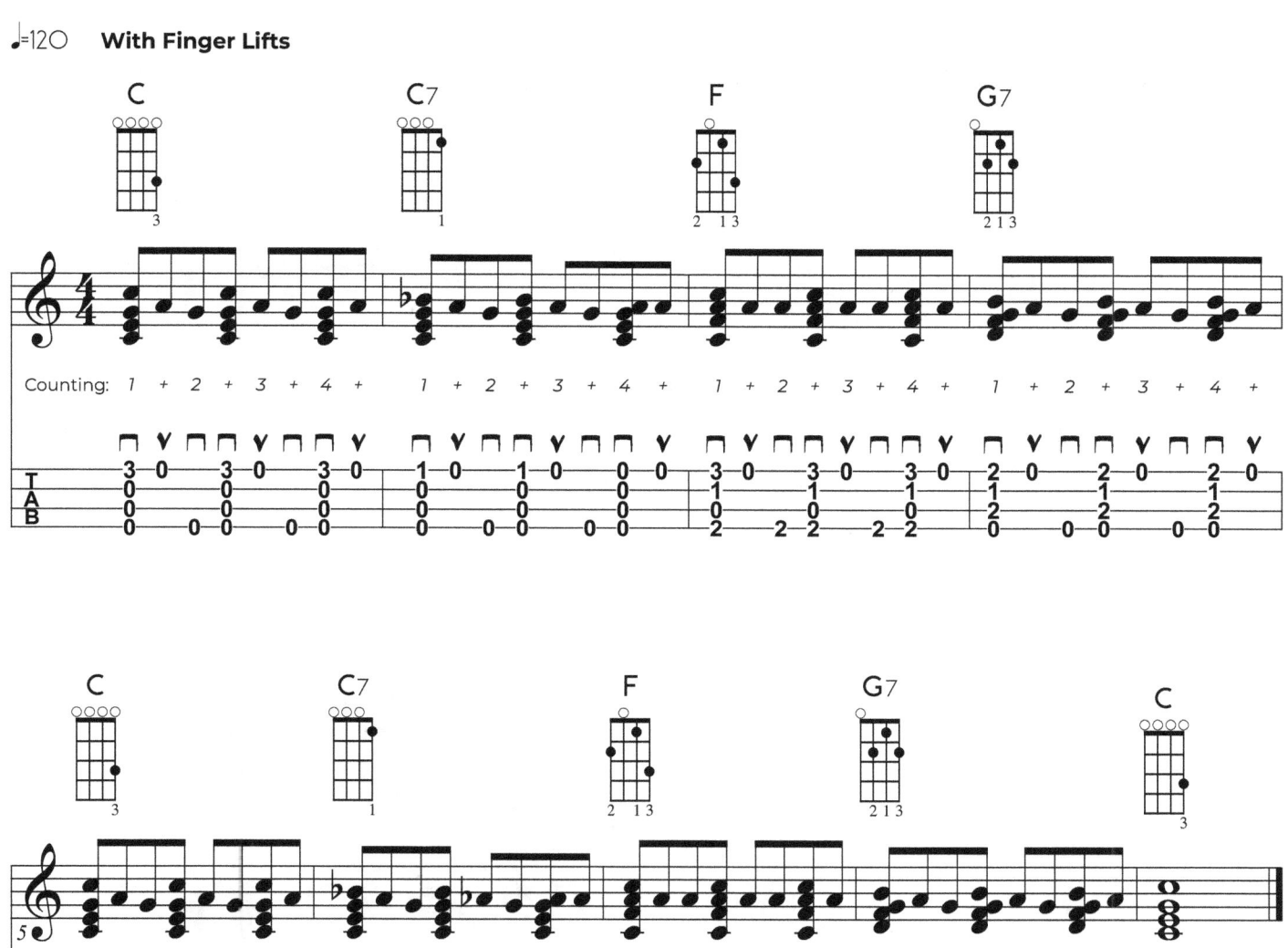

SWING ETUDE
A1 SECTION

In the first section of our etude we'll use our open position chords and focus on mixing up the strumming using triplets as well as our swung eighth notes. Remember that the strumming motion for all of the rhythms is the same, down and up, and let the triplets have the thumb follow through. The key is to start relaxed when we strum and let the rhythms bounce.

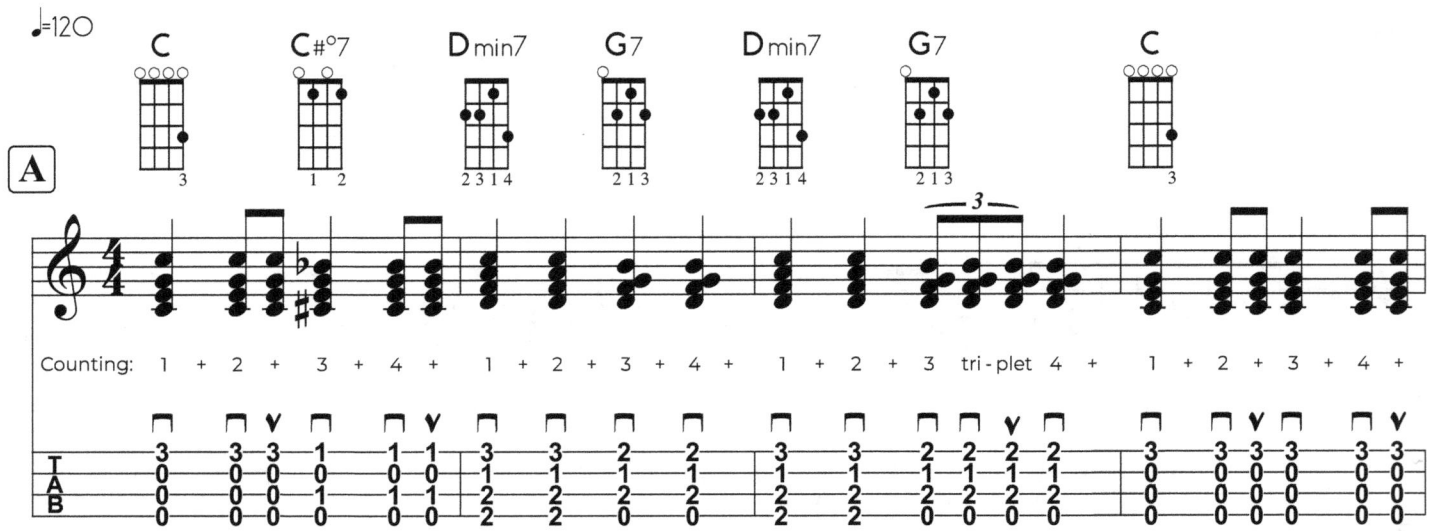

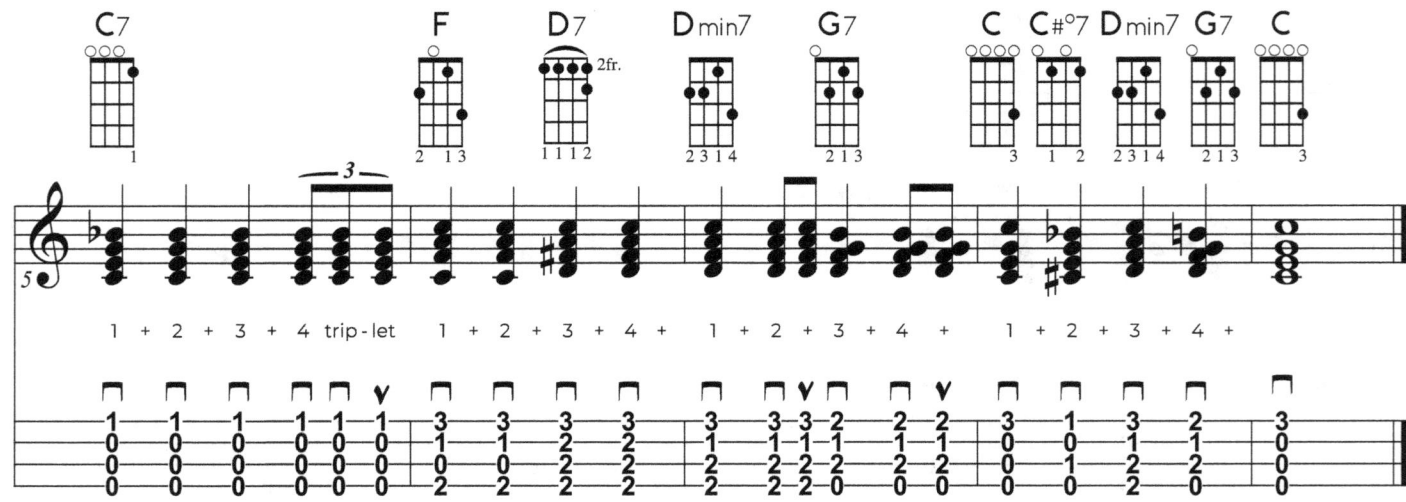

SWING ETUDE
A2 SECTION

In the second section of the etude we move to our closed position chords and try a few more rhythms as well as the split stroke. Now that we have our closed chords you can add in left hand muting on each down strum giving a little more groove to the quarter notes. Note the shuffle strum in bars 4 and 5 and don't let the split stroke in the last measure sneak up on you.

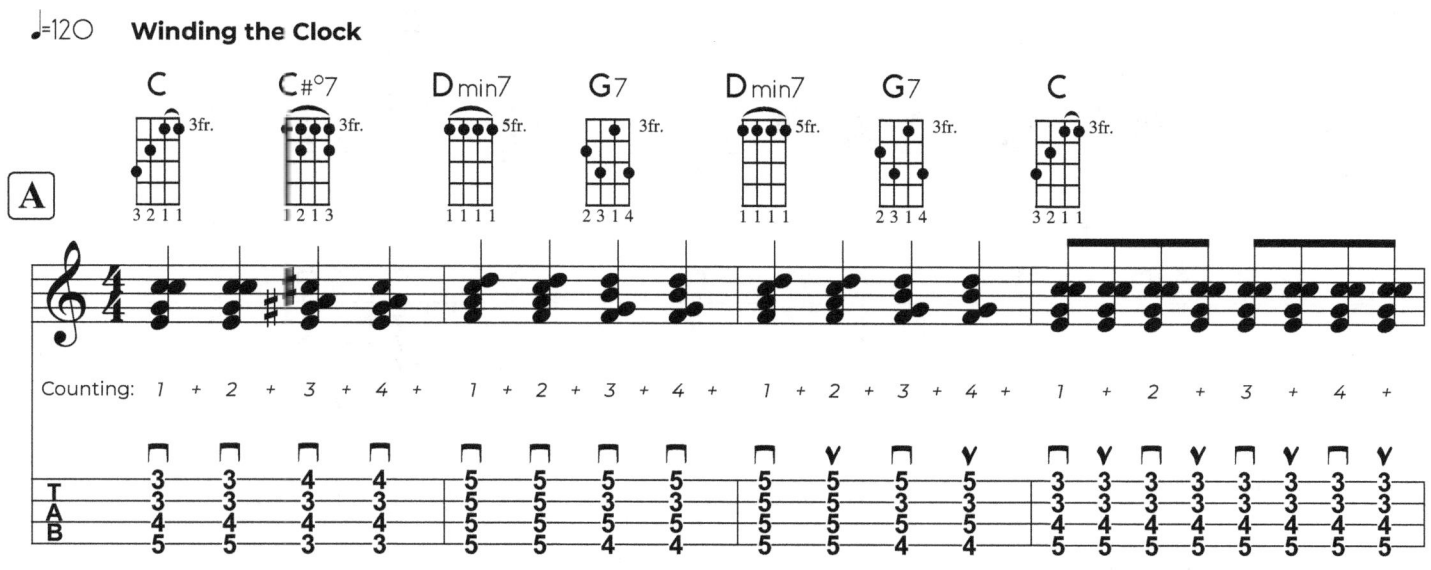

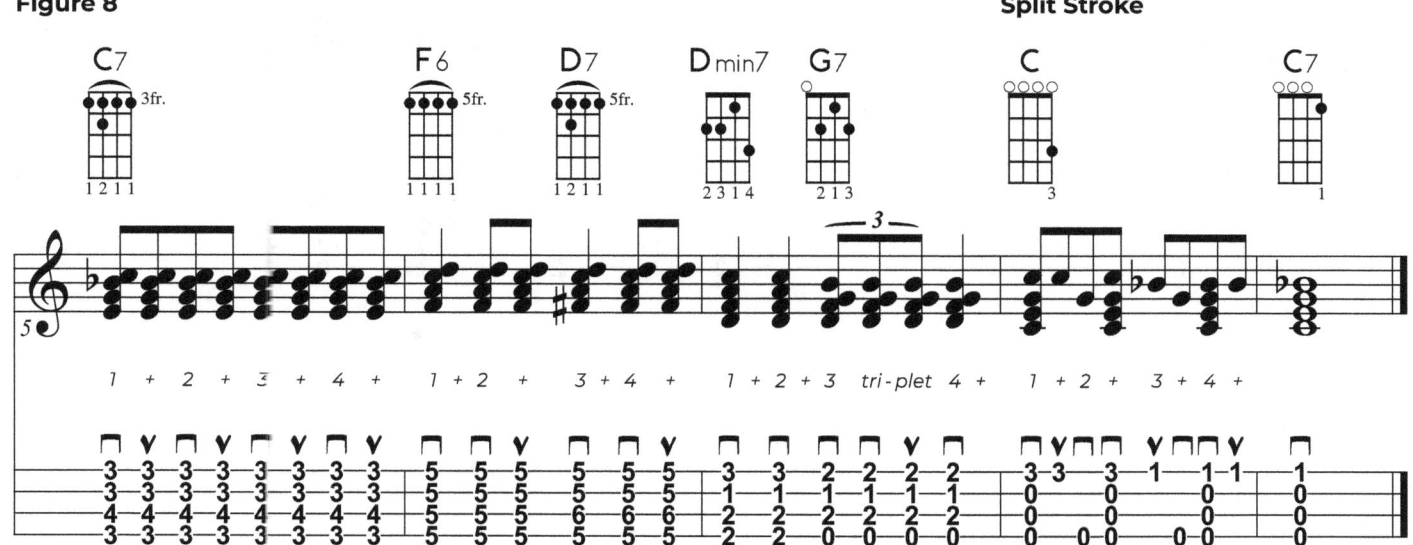

SWING ETUDE
B SECTION

Time to change up our chords a little bit with a few new ones up the neck. Try to strum through the chords first with all down strums before adding in the rhythms. All of our rhythms are now in this one 8 measure section and fly by fast. On the very last measure try to keep those triplets as even as possible to build momentum into the final A section.

SWING ETUDE
A3 SECTION

Now for a little bit of everything. In the final A section we mix up our open and closed position chords to create a little more movement in the harmony. In the last two measures we walk up to the grand finale by sliding up the G7 chord. For the harmonics on the very last beat, place your first finger lightly across the 12th fret and strum hard to make them really ring out.

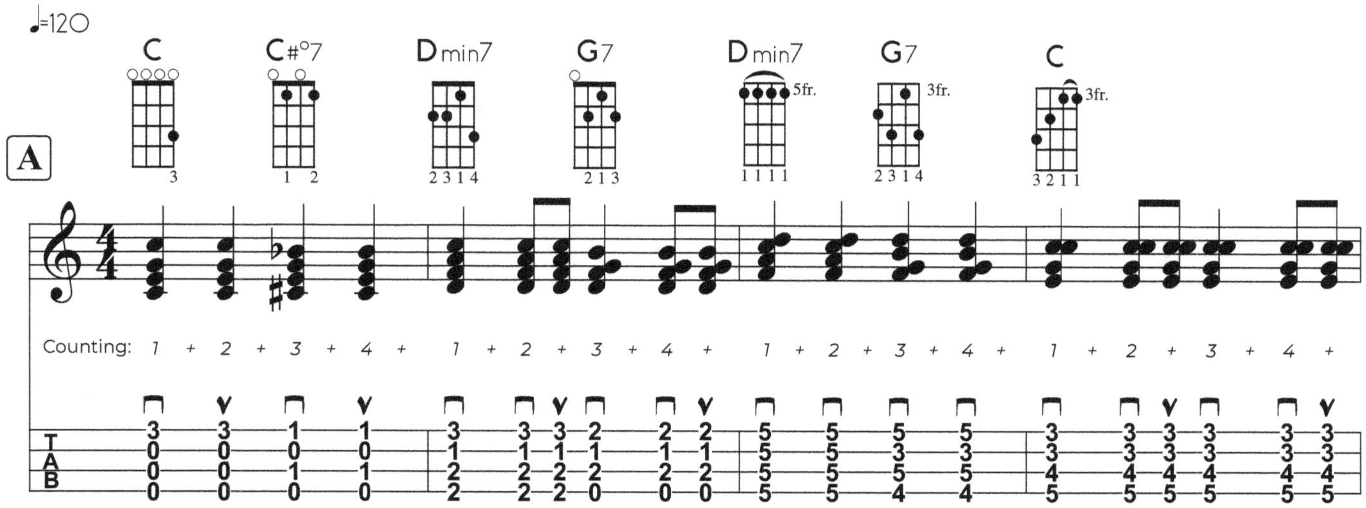

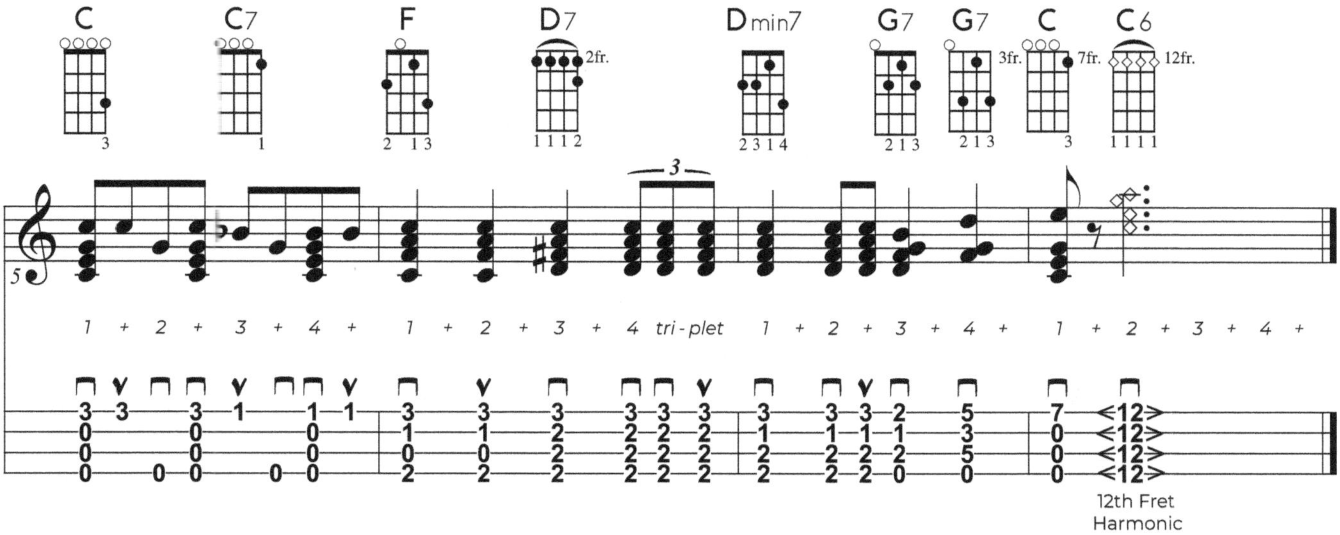

SWING ETUDE
PG. 1 of 3

Now let's put everything together to play the complete piece.

SWING ETUDE
PG. 2 of 3

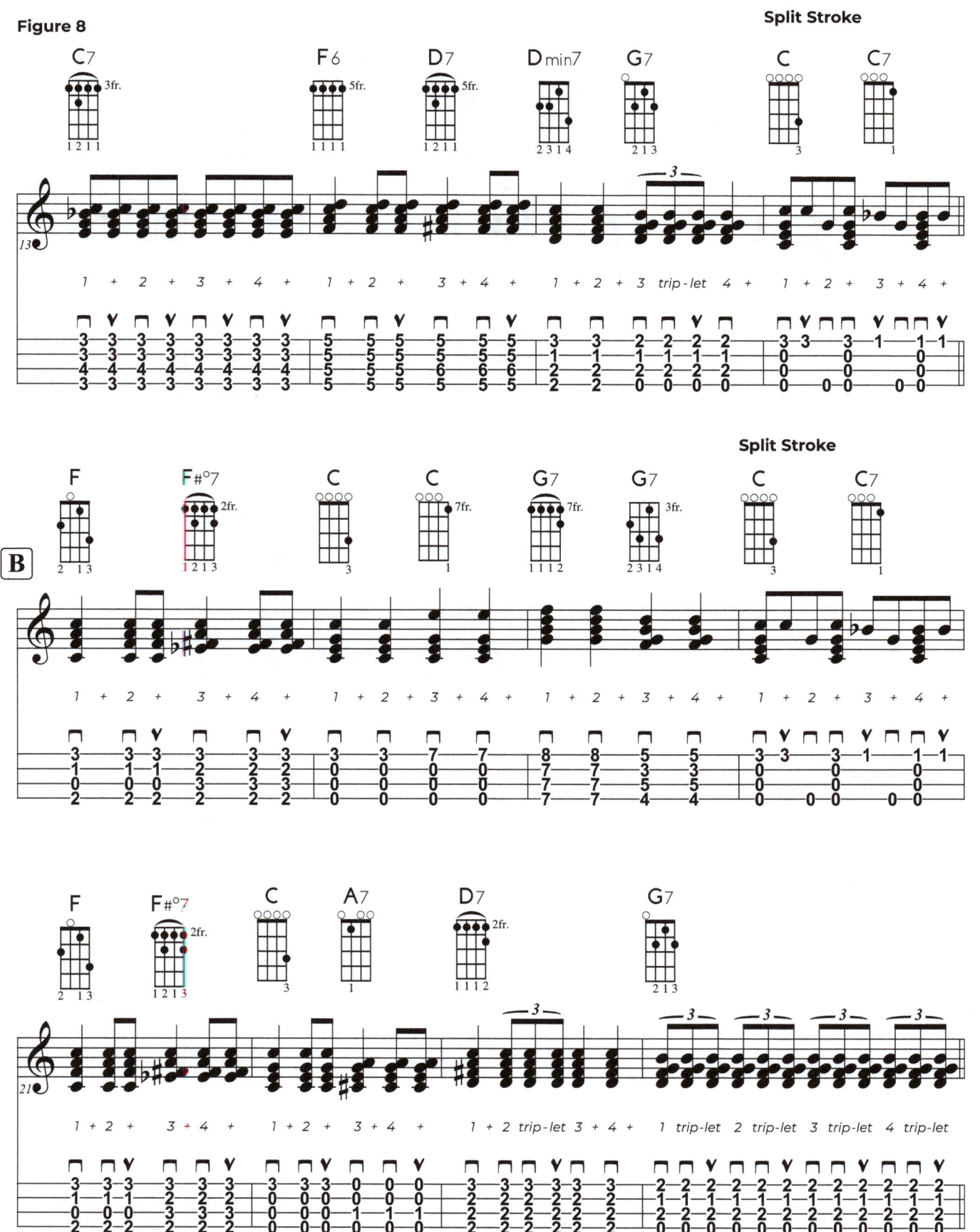

SWING ETUDE
PG. 3 of 3

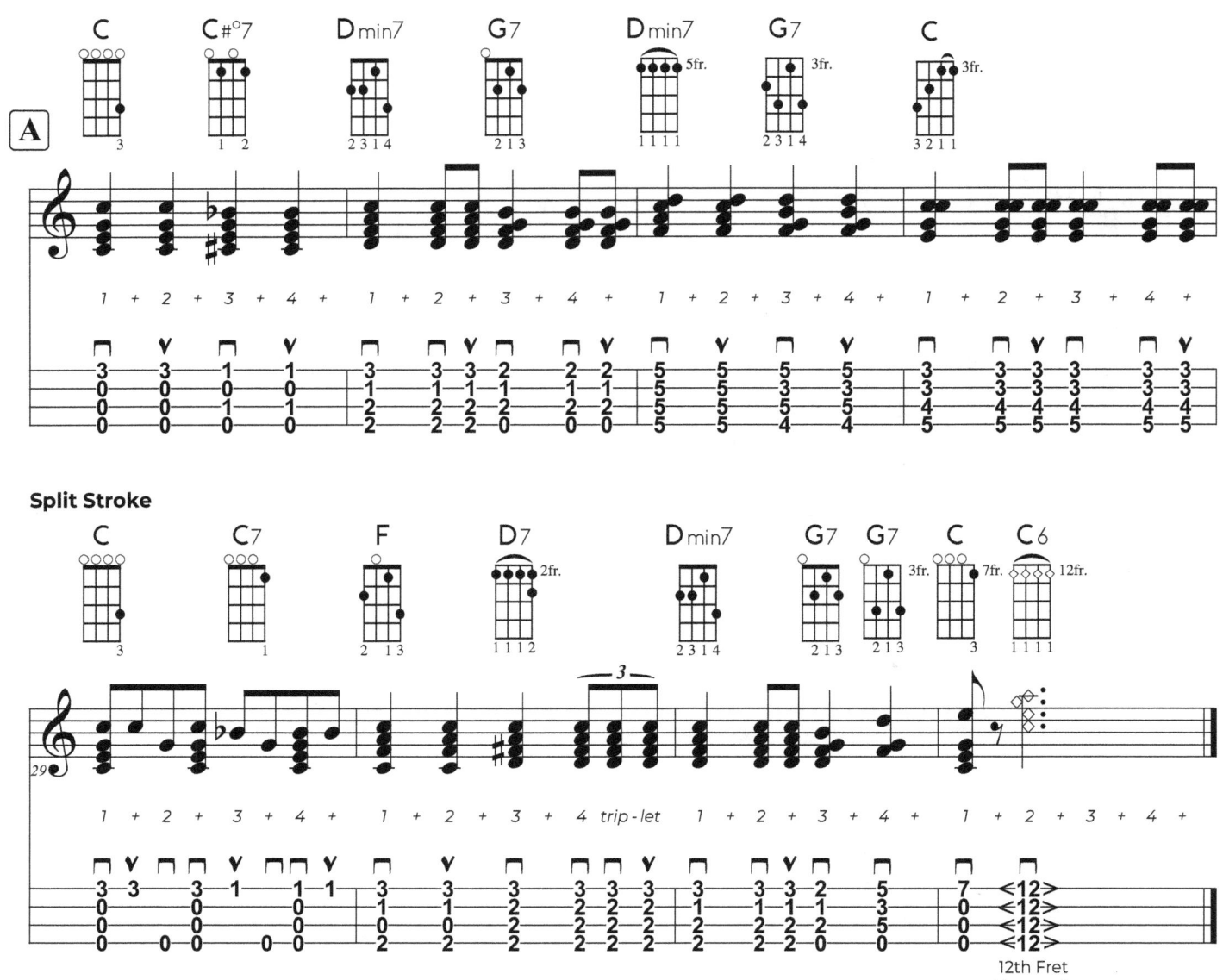

GREAT
JOB!

I want to congratulate you for getting through the Uke Like The Pros Jazz Ukulele Mastery Book 1. I am proud of you for making the commitment to yourself and your playing. You should now have a better understanding of Jazz Music, appreciate the unique jazzy rhythms and melodies, be a more skilled ukulele player, play with better timing, and feel more confident in your abilities.

Now that you are a Jazz Ukulele Master, it's time for you to take the next step in your playing by signing up for a FREE Month of the Platinum Membership. Platinum Members have access to over 25 Courses, Challenges, Giveaways, Workshops, and LIVE Q&A sessions with our members.

THE ESSENTIALS

It is important to learn and memorize these terms and symbols because they not only apply to ukulele but to all music.

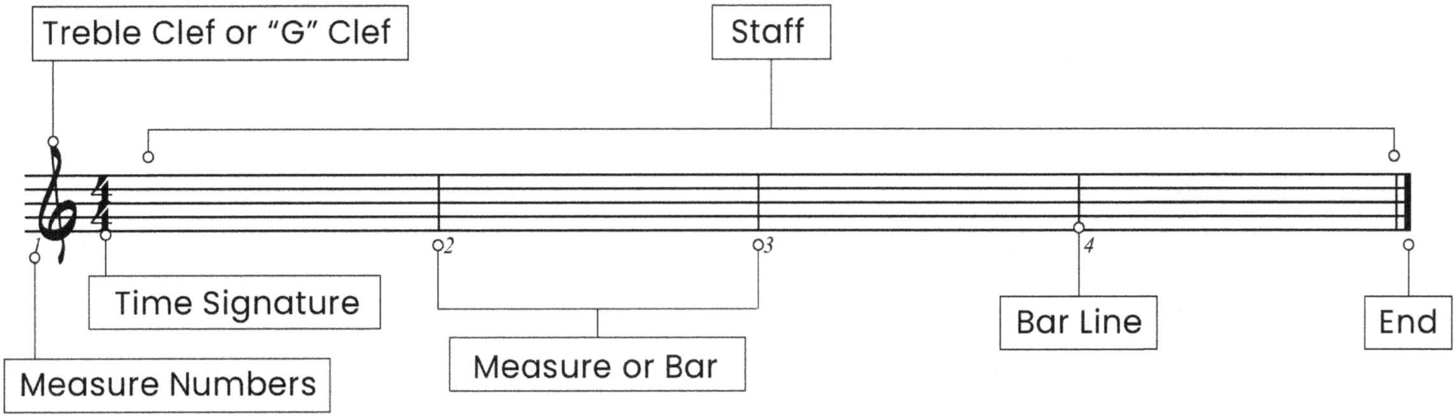

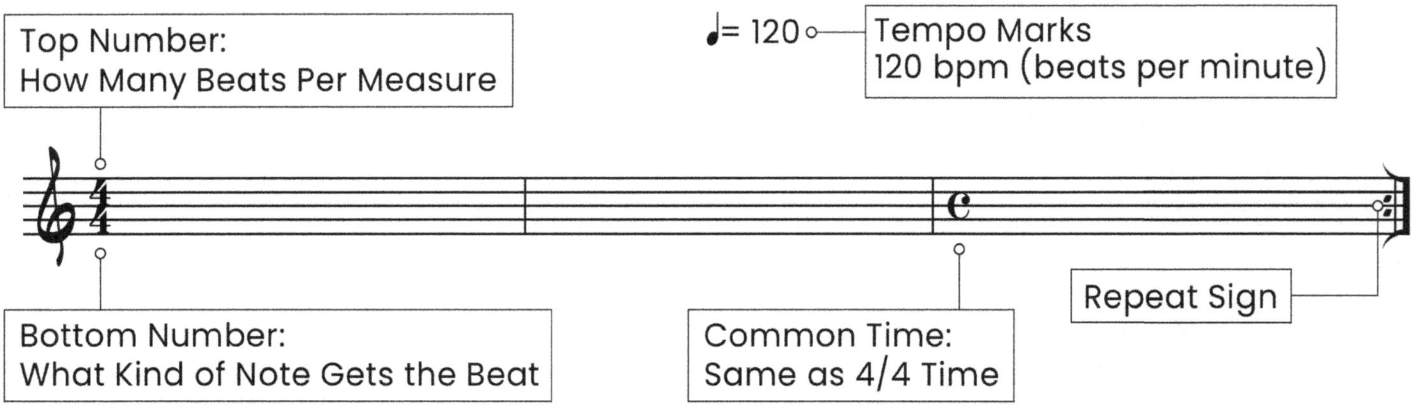

- Treble Clef or "G" Clef
- Staff
- Time Signature
- Measure Numbers
- Measure or Bar
- Bar Line
- End

- Top Number: How Many Beats Per Measure
- Tempo Marks: ♩= 120 — 120 bpm (beats per minute)
- Bottom Number: What Kind of Note Gets the Beat
- Common Time: Same as 4/4 Time
- Repeat Sign

Notes On The Staff: There are seven notes in music (A, B, C, D, E, F, G) and they move up and down alphabetically on the staff.

G A B C D E F G A B C D E F G A B C D E F

How To Remember The Notes:

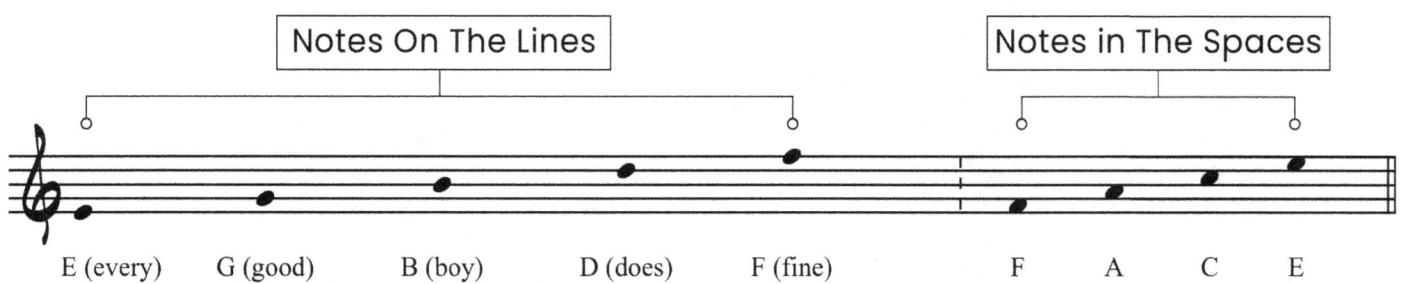

Notes On The Lines: E (every) G (good) B (boy) D (does) F (fine)

Notes in The Spaces: F A C E

HOW TO READ TAB

Tablature (TAB) is a form of music reading for ukulele that uses a 4 line staff and numbers. Each line of the staff represents a string on the ukulele and the numbers represent which fret you play on. When looking at the TAB staff it reads like it's upside down on the paper compared to the strings of your ukulele. On the TAB staff, the highest line (closest to the sky) represents the 1st string (A string) of the ukulele, while the lowest line (closest to the ground) represents the 4th string (G string) of the ukulele. When you see 2 or more notes stacked on top of each other on the TAB staff, that means you play those notes at the same time, like a a chord.

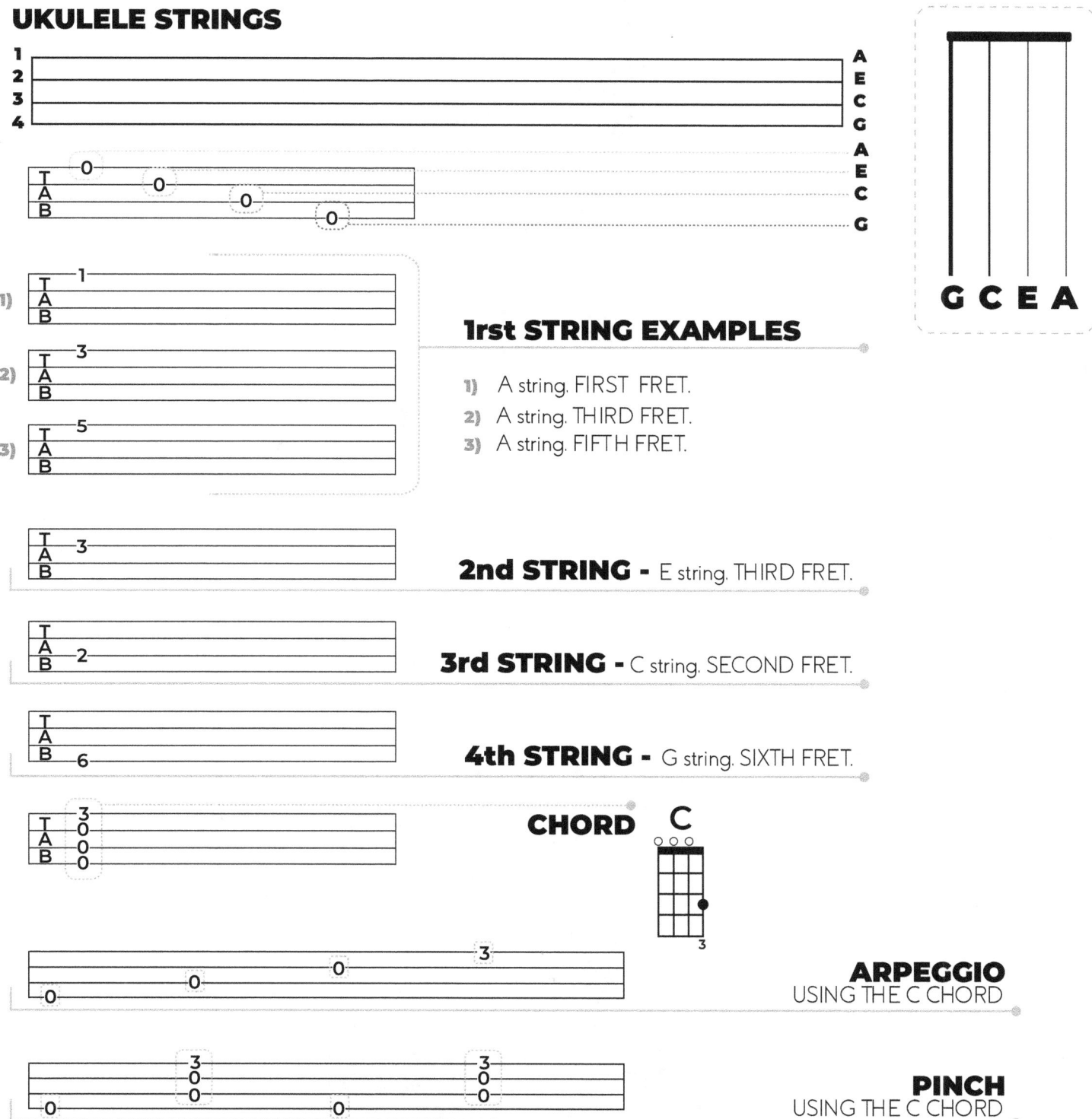

NOTES ON THE UKULELE NECK

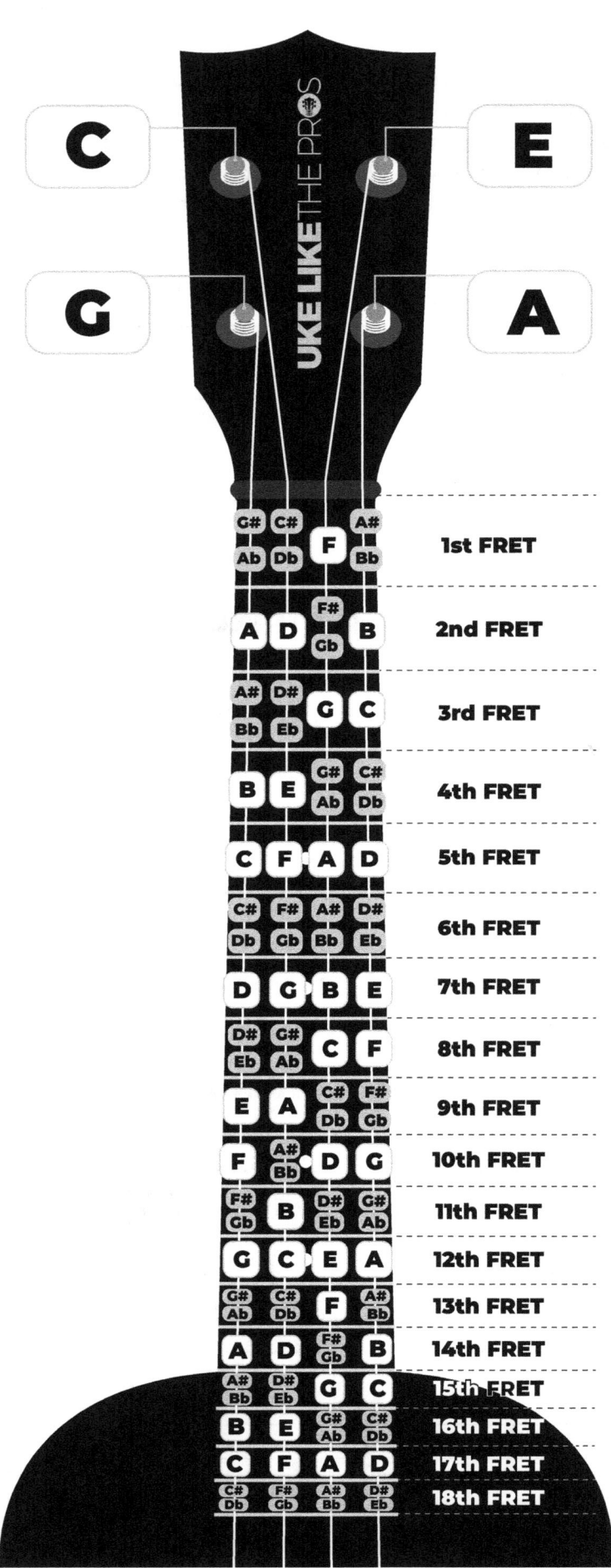

UKULELE HANDS

When playing fingerstyle on your ukulele, you will see both letters and numbers to indicate which fingers to use both for picking hand and your fretting hand. These letters and numbers will show up in the music notation, TAB, and chord diagrams.

FRETTING HAND
The left hand for right-handed players. will be indicated in the music or chord diagrams by numbers:
- **1**=Index finger
- **2**=Middle finger
- **3**=Ring finger
- **4**=Pinky finger

PICKING HAND
The right hand for right-handed players. will be indicated in the music by letters:
- **p**=Thumb
- **i**=Index
- **m**=Middle
- **a**=Ring
- **c**=Pinky (not used in this course)

LEFT — FRETTING HAND

RIGHT — PICKING HAND

UKULELE PARTS

UNDERSTANDING CHORD DIAGRAMS

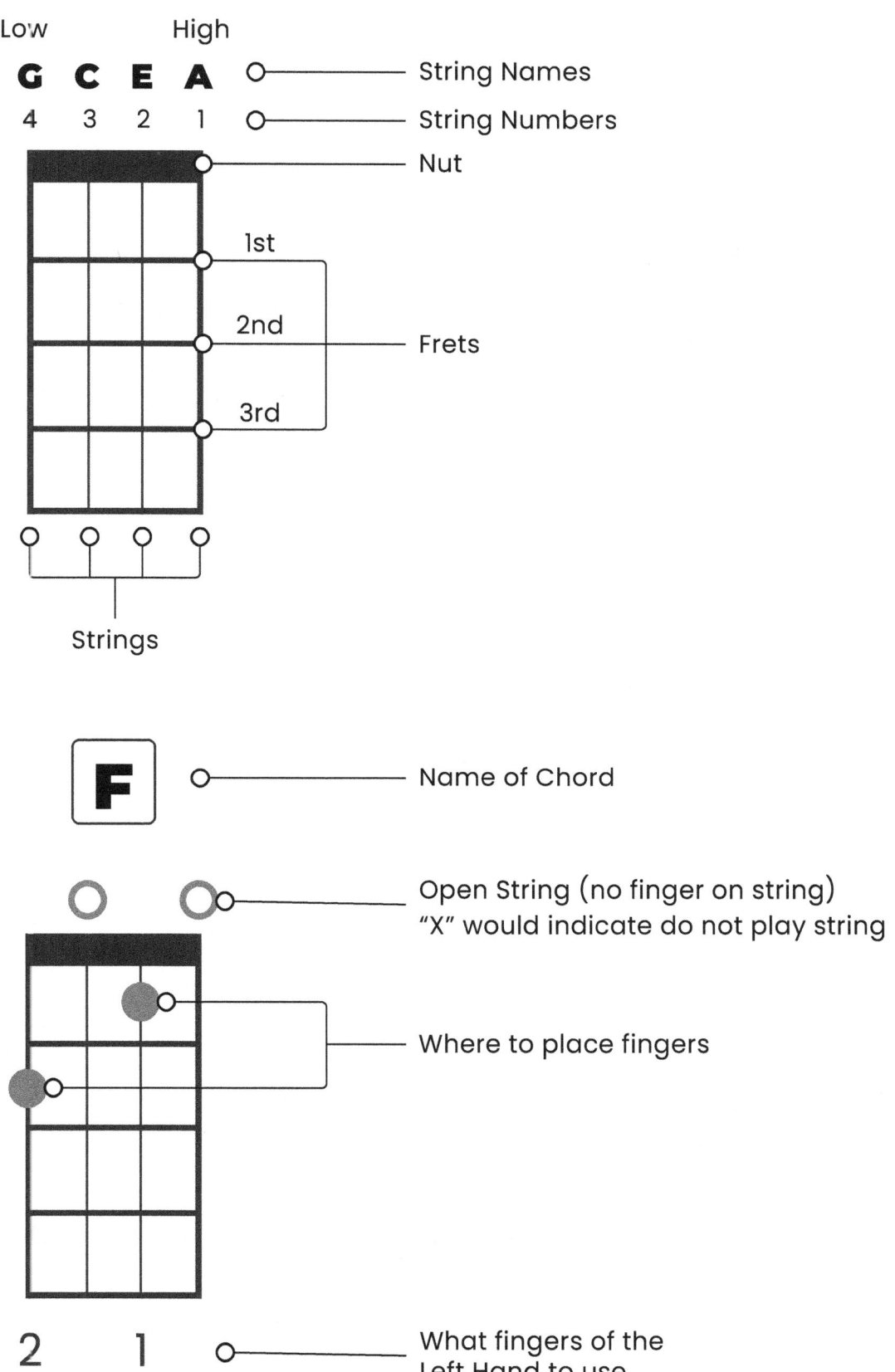

CHORD CHART

These are some of the most widely used chords in all of music. Although there are more chords that are listed, these chords represent the most widely used shapes.

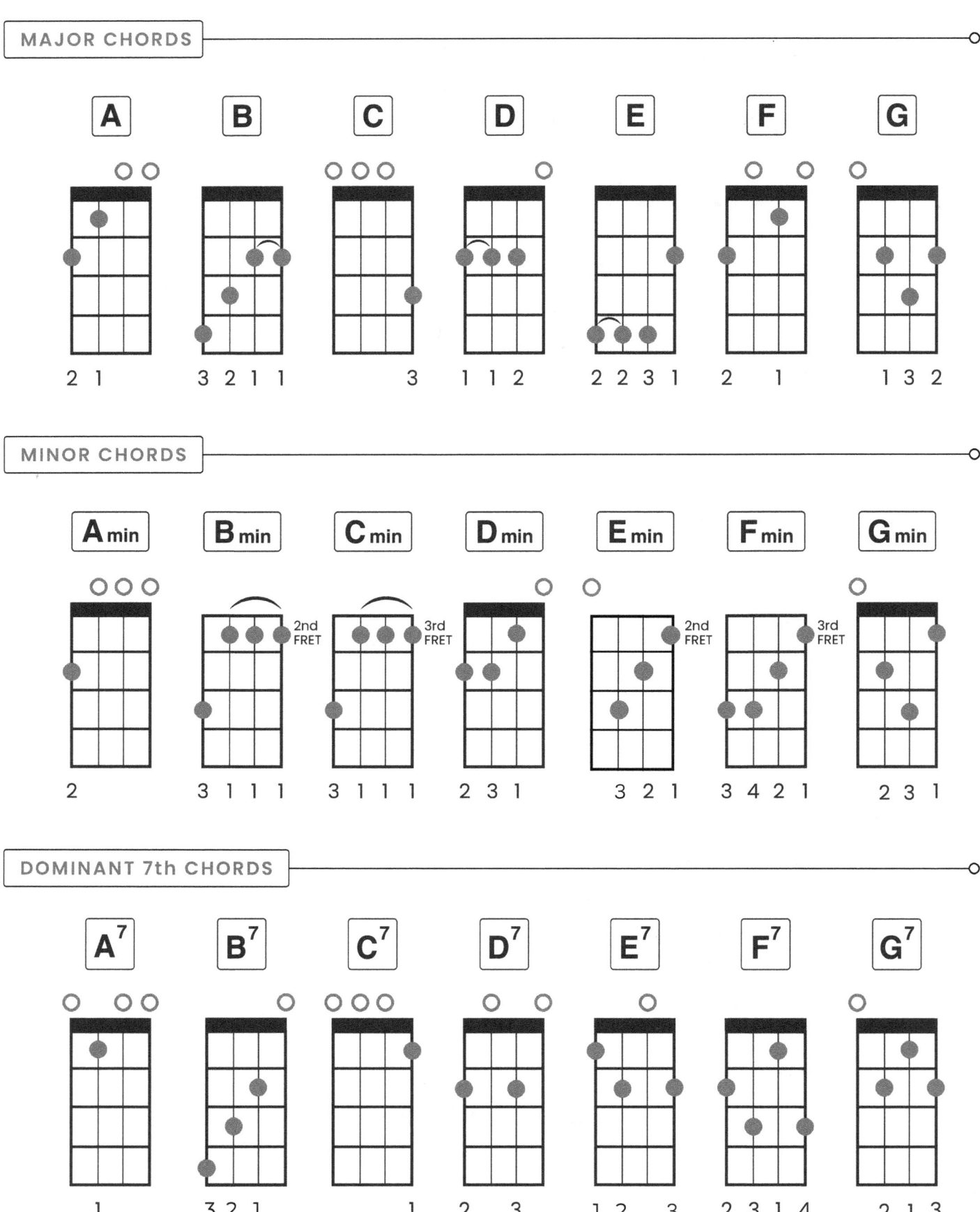

MAJOR 7th CHORDS

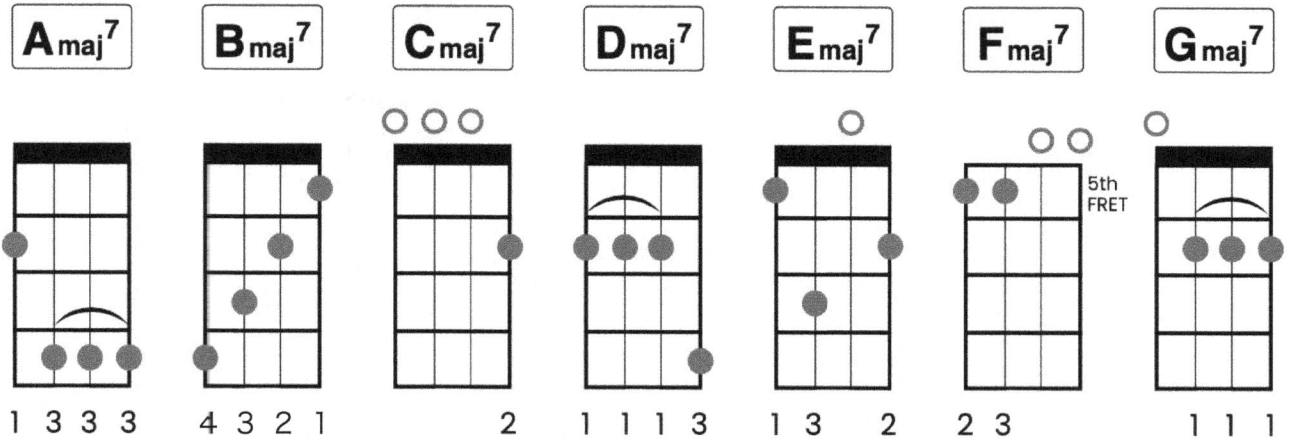

MINOR 7th CHORDS

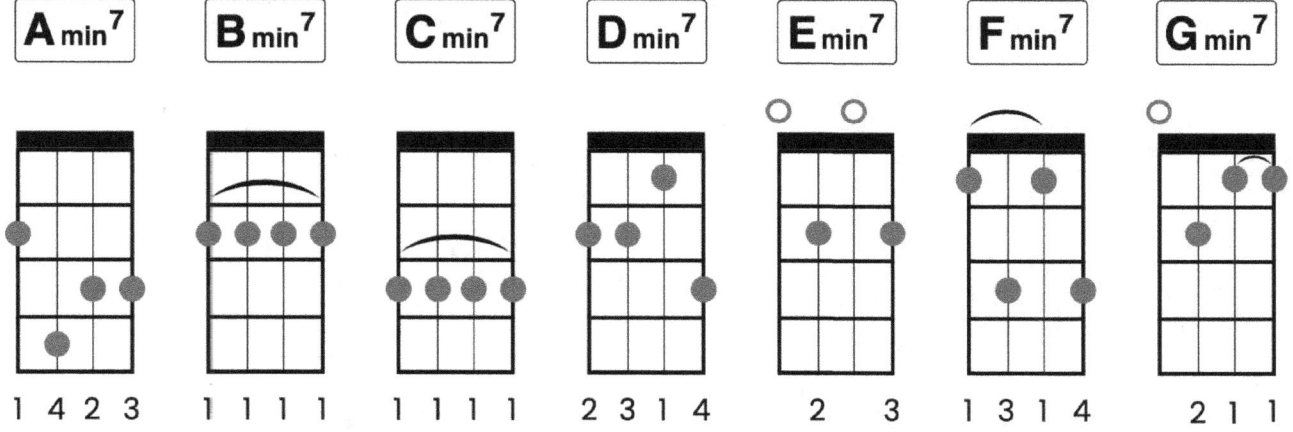

SUS + ADD CHORDS

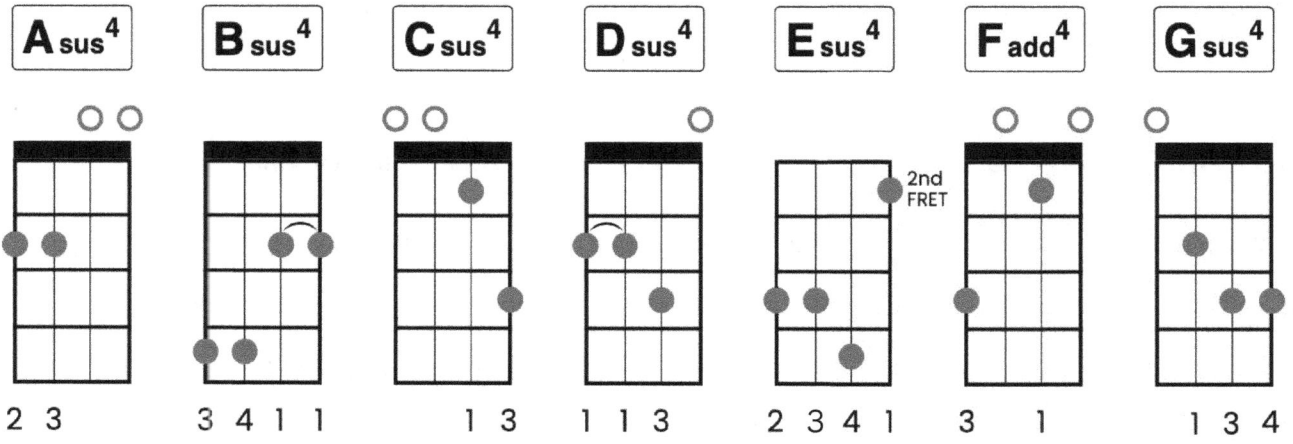

MUSIC SYMBOLS TO KNOW

A variety of symbols, articulations, repeats, hammer on's, pull off's, bends, and slides.

Fermata: Hold note

Staccato: Play note short

Accent: Play note loud

Accented Staccato: Play note loud + short

Vibrato: Rapid "shaking" of note

Arpeggiated Chord: Play the notes in fast succession from low to high strings

Grace Note: Fast embellishment note played before the main note

Mute: "Muffle" sound of strings either with left or right hand

Down Stroke: Pick string(s) with a downward motion

Up Stroke: Pick string(s) with an upward motion

Tie: Play first note but do not play second note that it is tied to

Ledger Lines: Extend the staff higher or lower.

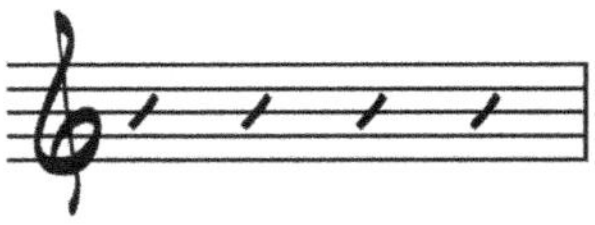

Slash Notation: Repeat notes & rhythms from previous measure

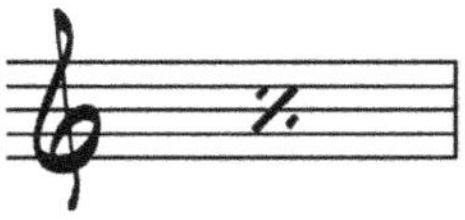

1 Bar Repeat: Repeat notes & rhythms from previous measure

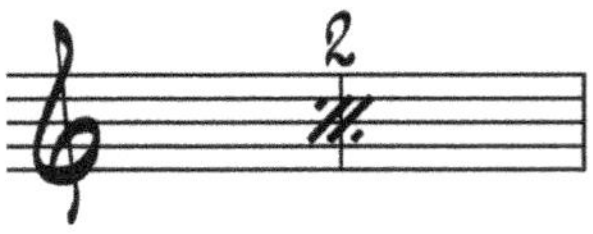

2 Bar Repeat: Repeat notes & rhythms from previous 2 measures

Repeat Sign: (Beginning)

Repeat Sign: (End)

1st Ending: Play this part the first time only

2nd Ending: Play this part the second time

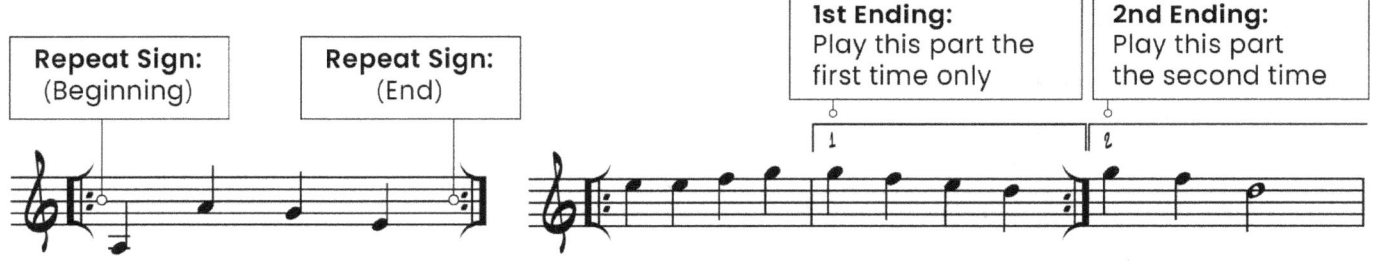

(D.C. AL FINE) — *D.C.* (da capo) means go to the beginning of the tune and stop when you get to *Fine*

(D.C. AL CODA) — *D.C.* means go to the beginning of the tune and jump to *Coda* ⊕ when you see the sign ⊕

(D.S. AL FINE) — *D.S.* (dal segno) means go to the *Sign* 𝄋 and stop when you get to *Fine*

(D.S. AL CODA) — *D.S.* means go to the *Sign* 𝄋 And Jump to the *Coda* ⊕ when you see ⊕

SIM... — Play the same rhythm, strum pattern, or picking pattern as the previous measure

ETC... — Continue the same rhythm, strum pattern, or picking pattern as the previous measure

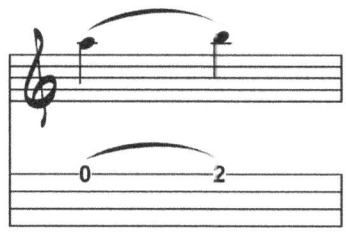

Hammer On:
Pick first note then hammer on to the next note without picking it.

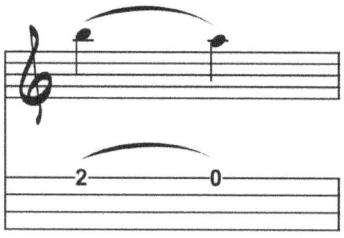

Pull Off:
Pick first note then pull off to the next note without picking it.

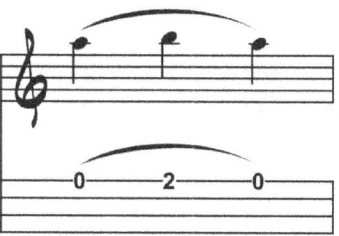

Hammer On & Pull Off:
Pick first note, hammer on to the next note, and pull off to the last note all in one motion.

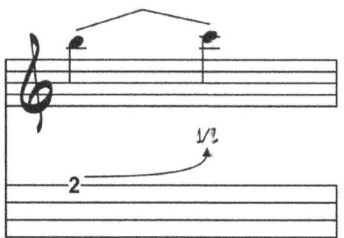

1/2 Step Bend:
Bend the first note a 1/2 step or 1 fret.

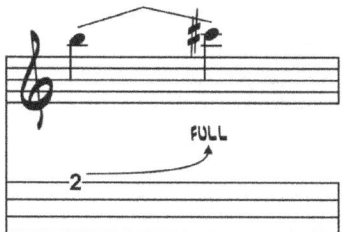

Whole Step Bend:
Bend the first note a whole step or 2 frets.

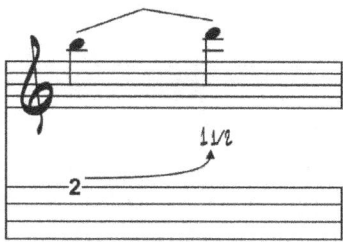

Step & 1/2 Bend:
Bend the first note 1 1/2 steps or 3 frets.

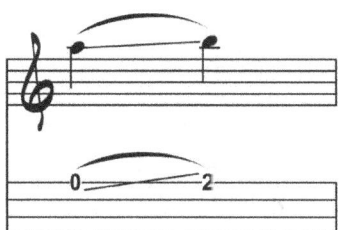

Forward Slide:
Pick first note and slide up to higher note.

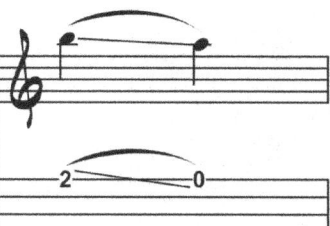

Backward Slide:
Pick first note and slide back to lower note.

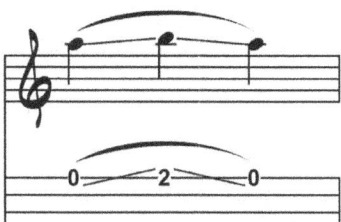

Forward/Backward Slide:
Pick first note, slide up to next note and then slide back.

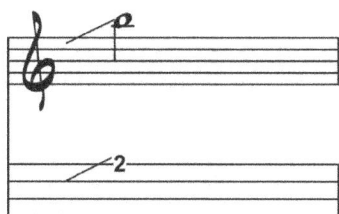

Slide Into Note:
Slide from 2-3 frets below note.

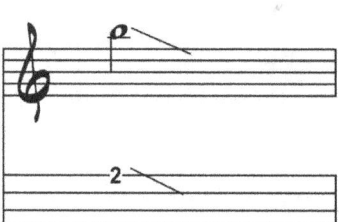

Slide Off Note:
Slide off 2-5 frets after note.

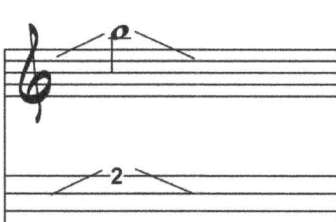

Slide Into Note then Slide Off Note.

ABOUT THE PUBLISHER

Terry Carter is a San Diego-based ukulele player, surfer, songwriter, and creator of ukelikethepros.com, rocklikethepros.com and terrycartermusicstore.com. With over 25 years as a professional musician, educator and Los Angeles studio musician, Terry has worked with greats like Weezer, Josh Groban, Robby Krieger (The Doors), 2-time Grammy winning composer Christopher Tin (Calling All Dawns), Duff McKagan (Guns N' Roses), Grammy winning producer Charles Goodan (Santana/Rolling Stones), and the Los Angeles Philharmonic. Terry has written and produced tracks for commercials (Discount Tire and Puma) and TV shows, including Scorpion (CBS), Pit Bulls & Parolees (Animal Planet), Trippin', Wildboyz, and The Real World (MTV). He has self-published over 25 books for Uke Like The Pros and Rock Like The Pros, filmed over 30 ukulele and guitar online courses, and has millions of views on his social media channels. Terry received a Master of Music in Studio/Jazz Guitar Performance from University of Southern California and a Bachelor of Music from San Diego State University, with an emphasis in Jazz Studies and Music Education. He has taught at the University of Southern California, San Diego State University, Santa Monica College, Miracosta College, and Los Angeles Trade Tech College.

ONLINE UKULELE COURSES

The perfect place to learn how to play Ukulele, Baritone Ukulele, Guitar and Guitarlele.

ULTP Roadmap
WHERE TO START?

1) UKULELE BEGINNER
- A. Beginning Ukulele Starter Course
- B. Beginning Ukulele Bootcamp Course
- C. Ukulele Fundamentals Course
- D. Ukulele Practice & Technique Course
- E. Master the Ukulele 1

2) UKULELE INTERMEDIATE
- A. Master The Ukulele 2
- B. Beginning Music Reading
- C. 23 Ultimate Chord Progressions
- D. Beginning Ukulele Fingerstyle Course

3) UKULELE ADVANCED
- A. Ukulele Blues Mastery Course
- B. Beginning Ukulele Soloing Course
- C. Fingerstyle Mastery Course
- D. Jazz Swing Mastery Course

MORE OPTIONS!

FUNLAND
- A. Beginning Ukulele Kids Course Songbook
- B. 21 Popular Songs for Ukulele
- C. The Best Ukulele Christmas Songs
- D. 10 Classic Rock Licks
- E. Guitar Fundamentals

BARITONE UKULELE
- A. Beginning Baritone Ukulele Bootcamp Course
- B. 6 Weeks Baritone Q&A
- C. Baritone Blues Mastery Course
- D. Beginning Baritone Fingerstyle Course

GUITARLELE
- A. Guitarlele Starter Course
- B. 6 Weeks Guitarlele Q&A
- C. Guitarlele Course for Ukulele and Guitar Players
- D. Guitarlele Blues Mastery Course

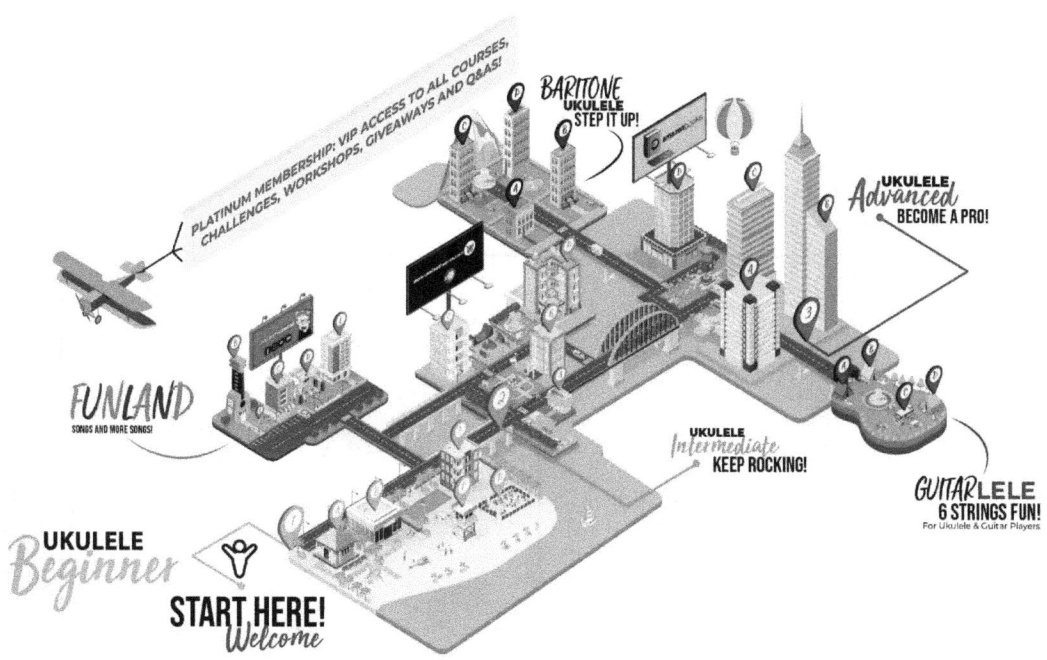

Courses For All Levels
UKELIKETHEPROS.COM

TERRY CARTER MUSIC STORE

All your music needs at the #1 music store, **terrycartermusicstore.com**

Baritones

Ukuleles

Guitars

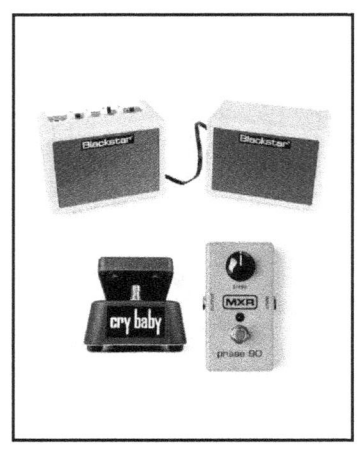

Amplifiers and Pedals

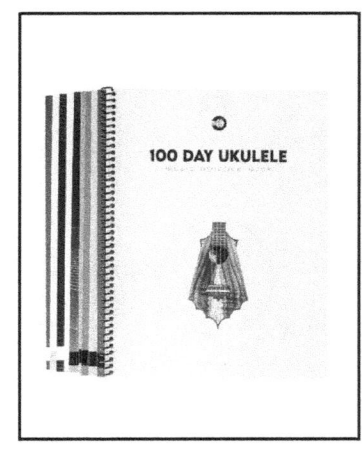

Books

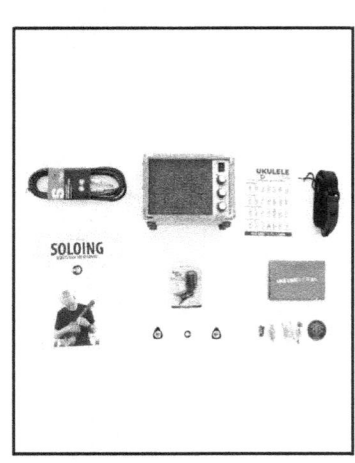

Accessories

UKELIKETHEPROS.COM
BLOG.UKELIKETHEPROS.COM
TERRYCARTERMUSICSTORE.COM
BUYSTRINGSONLINE.COM

@ukelikethepros

INTERESTED IN **GUITAR CONTENT?**
ROCKLIKETHEPROS.COM

www.ingramcontent.com/pod-product-compliance
Lightning Source LLC
Chambersburg PA
CBHW081356040426
42451CB00017B/3474